T H E
BEAUTIF
BODY BOOK

T H E
BEAUTIFUL
BODY BOOK

A Lifetime Guide for Healthy, Younger-Looking Skin

ZIA WESLEY-HOSFORD

BANTAM BOOKS
TORONTO · NEW YORK · LONDON · SYDNEY · AUCKLAND

NOTE

This book discusses certain drugs, vitamins, health and beauty products, and various treatments and procedures that may be beneficial for some individuals' conditions and problems, but which may also have negative side effects in other individuals. Before undergoing any treatment or procedure, and before starting any drug, exercise, or vitamin program, you should consult with your own personal physician who can counsel you about your own specific needs.

All photographs on pages 82 and 83 are from
CALLANETICS: Ten Years Younger in Ten Hours by Callan
Pinckney. Copyright © 1984 by Callan Pinckney.
Reprinted by permission of William Morrow, Inc.

THE BEAUTIFUL BODY BOOK
A Bantam Book / March 1989

Library of Congress Cataloging-in-Publication Data

Wesley-Hosford, Zia.
  The beautiful body book.

  1. Skin-Care and hygiene.   2. Beauty, Personal.
I. Title.
RL87.W47   1989   646.7'26   88-47822
ISBN 0-553-34622-9

Published simultaneously in the United States and Canada

*Bantam Books are published by Bantam Books, a division of Bantam
Doubleday Dell Publishing Group, Inc. Its trademark, consisting of the words
"Bantam Books" and the portrayal of a rooster, is Registered in U.S. Patent
and Trademark Office and in other countries. Marca Registrada. Bantam
Books, 666 Fifth Avenue, New York, New York 10103.*

PRINTED IN THE UNITED STATES OF AMERICA

FG   0 9 8 7 6 5 4 3 2 1

*This book is dedicated in loving memory
to my friend and editor, Tobi Sanders.*

CONTENTS

INTRODUCTION: ALL ABOUT SKIN

The skin that covers our bodies is very much alive. Like other major organs of the body, it continually functions, performing a myriad of duties. In fact, the skin is our largest organ, weighing twice as much as the brain and covering a total average area of 21 square feet. Aside from its obvious function of covering muscles, bones, and other organs, and protecting them from the invasion of bacteria, the skin helps regulate the body's air conditioning and heating systems. Skin takes in a portion of the oxygen that is necessary for the production of new cells, blood, and plasma, and continually releases toxic waste through sweat glands and pores. In addition, it manufactures sebum—the body's natural moisturizer.

Located throughout the skin are millions of sensory nerve endings which give us our sense of touch and send warning signals to the brain and other organs. Skin is vital to the life of the body. We could not exist without it. (Try to imagine for a moment what life would be like if you were missing just a few inches of skin from any part of your body.) Skin is one of the few major organs that researchers have not been able to duplicate in a laboratory. We have artificial hearts, replacements for colons and kidneys, and operations that enable food to bypass the stomach. A person can readily survive with one lung. But without our skin we can't live even close to a normal life. All things considered, it's hard to understand why so many people treat their skin as if it were totally inconsequential; as if it could be easily replaced.

One of the most amazing features of the skin is its ability to heal itself. Unfortunately, it may be this ability that gives people the idea that the skin can take care of itself, and to a point, it can. The skin continues to function, as best it can, despite our abuse and neglect. Imagine how much healthier and more attractive it might be if it were treated properly.

As with many other things, many people don't start to care for their skin until it gives them trouble. This usually occurs after 30, when signs of age begin to appear. Abuse and neglect, like the ravages of too much sun, tend to have a cumulative effect. When we are young the skin is forgiving and always seems able to recover (and we take it for granted). Suddenly, as we approach mid-life, it begins to look dry, cracked, lined, baggy, scarred, rough, or discolored. Evidence of skin cancer, a direct result of sun exposure, appears in one out of every three Americans over the age of 30. Years of abuse and indifference have taken their toll. The bad news is that most of these symptoms could have been avoided with better lifetime care. The good news is that, regardless of what stage your skin is in, real improvement can *always* be made.

In order to treat and care for the skin properly, it is important to know how it works. The cells that make up the outer layer of skin, or epidermis, are dead. They are the end result of a 28-day cycle of birth, growth, and death that begins in the dermis, or lower layer of the skin. When new cells are born, they are round and filled with fluid. As they make their way toward the surface of the skin, they lose their fluid, becoming elongated and flat. Once the cells reach the outer layer of the skin, they fall off as a result of washing or rubbing. These cells are continually replaced by others that have made the same journey to the surface. If you have ever noticed a scaly look to your skin, you are actually seeing the buildup of dead, dry cells. This most often appears on the lower legs. As we get older, the shedding, or exfoliating, process slows down and our skin begins to need help to rid itself of these cells. Without our assistance, the scaly buildup so often associated with age will persist.

The dermis, or lower layer, is made up of collagen and elastin protein fibers. These fibers comprise the "skeleton" of the skin, similar to a mesh netting. Without them, the skin would lack its ability to stretch and be resilient. Dr. Alan Gaynor, a cosmetic dermatologist in San Francisco and an expert in the use of collagen implantation, describes collagen as "a microscopic network of fibers woven together like threads in a fabric." As gravity, facial expressions, and ultraviolet light begin to take their toll on these fibers, the skin begins to line, wrinkle, sag, and show other signs of age. Simultaneously (as we age), production of these fibers also slows down. Although no cream or lotion can replenish these fibers, even those that contain collagen and elastin, there are several other ways to boost their production and protect them from breakdown. The various methods of accomplishing this will be discussed throughout this book.

Within the collagen/elastin network of fibers are sebaceous glands, which manufacture and secrete sebum. This substance, so vital to the health and beauty of the skin, is actually a mixture of oil and water. It is the skin's natural lubricant, or moisturizer. Once it has combined with sweat to form an emulsion, it resembles a commercial moisturizer. As we age, sebum production slows down, and without this natural lubrication, the skin dries out, develops fine lines, and may even crack. However, often the slowdown may be attributed to bad habits that we've adopted, rather than some inevitable body process. Experiments have proven that people who remain physically active and eat a diet high in vitamins A, E, and C continue to have adequate sebum production. (I will discuss the effect of diet on the skin in depth in Chapter 2.)

Also nestled among the collagen/elastin fibers of the dermis are sweat glands, blood vessels, hair follicles, and nerve endings. Each is dependent upon the healthy maintenance of the epidermis in order to function properly. For example, if the epidermis is clogged by a buildup of dead cells, sweat can become trapped beneath the skin. Sweat contains a toxic waste that is meant to be eliminated from the body, and if trapped, may cause breakouts. Likewise, trapped sebum causes whiteheads and skin bumps. Hair follicles that become encrusted with a buildup of dead skin cells cause a condition known as keratosis pilaris. This condition is characterized by tiny, hard bumps on the skin that appear most often on the upper arms and thighs. (The treatment of this condition is described in Chapter 9.)

In some instances, problems caused by overexposure to the sun, weight gain and loss, lack of exercise, and overindulgence in abusive substances such as alcohol and cigarettes may seem irreparable. However, even problems such as these may be improved greatly through proper nutrition, supplemental vitamins, exercise, daily skin care, and appropriate use of cosmetics. More severe problems may also be ultimately corrected by various means of cosmetic surgery. These treatments are discussed in depth throughout the book.

It is no coincidence that a healthy body is a beautiful one. Any treatment that improves the health of the body will also enhance its esthetic beauty. This book will help you improve the health and beauty of your body and the skin that covers it.

Why I Do What I Do

After I received my license in cosmetology at the Vidal Sassoon Academy in San Francisco and trained for two months at a facial salon in Beverly Hills, I began my own facial business at Dorlane Hair Design in Sausalito. This everyday contact with skin and the products and techniques that improve it piqued my curiosity. I wondered: What made people break out? How and why did stress affect the skin? What were all those chemicals listed on the back labels of products? Did diet, chemicals, cigarettes, exercise, and sun exposure make a difference to the skin? Why did some products work well while others made people break out?

As I began the search for the answers to these and other questions, I uncovered a veritable Pandora's box. Finding the answers was extremely difficult since no available information existed. Cosmetic companies gave no information other than that stated in advertisements, and manufacturers led me to believe that all cosmetics are basically the same. Manufacturers and sellers of "natural" cosmetics wanted me to believe that all chemicals were harmful, while dermatologists claimed that it didn't matter what you put on your skin provided that you put cream on if it was dry, or something, like alcohol, to dry it out if it was oily. Nutritionists were the most helpful by actually making a connection between the ingestion of nutrients and good or bad skin.

In the following years, as my clientele grew, I was able to answer many of my questions through experience and observation. I could look at people's skin and tell what types of products they did or did not use, how much water they drank, if they ate a lot of dairy products, if they smoked cigarettes, what side of their body they slept on, how much stress they were under, and how much sun exposure they had had throughout their life. I began to put this experience to practical use and to warn people to stay out of the sun as a way of preventing facial aging. I took people off products containing mineral oil and watched their faces clear up. I changed people's diets and product regimens and saw that their skin became less oily and more balanced. The results were many—better skin, money saved by avoiding products that didn't work, simplified skin care routines, and fewer breakouts. I even successfully treated acne with diet and product modification, in place of antibiotics and drying lotions. In *The Beautiful Body Book* I'll be sharing the results of years of research and practice with you.

How I Do What I Do

I test a product by first reading the ingredient label and analyzing its formulation. If I find something questionable or unfamiliar, I consult with a cosmetic chemist. If I suspect that one or more ingredients may have been deleted from a label, I send the product to a cosmetic chemist for analysis. If a product does not meet my standards of composition, no further testing is required and the product is eliminated.

If a product is well made, I test it next by using it myself. Provided I do not have any adverse reaction, I then send a sample of the product, along with a product information questionnaire, to three people of different ages and skin types. After using the product as directed, each person returns the completed questionnaire. The people who test products for me are all longtime clients, which gives me familiarity with their skin and habits. In this way, I know that they have good skin care habits and I can rely on them to follow directions and use products correctly. Familiarity also enables me to relate their reactions to their particular skin type. Very often a product will work for one type and not for another; this is something that comes out in testing. This collected information allows me to make educated and reliable recommendations about products for a variety of consumers, and you, my readers.

C H A P T E R
ONE

DO OUR MINDS
CONTROL
OUR BODIES?

Before telling you how to reprogram yourself for extended youth, I would like to share a personal experience with you.

When I turned 32, I began to notice some things about my body and skin that I didn't like. Having been a sun worshipper and lived on the beach at Malibu for eight years, my face was beginning to show signs of sun damage: laugh lines around my eyes, loss of elasticity, and a change in the skin's texture and smoothness. I hadn't practiced a regular exercise program for two years because of a degenerative knee condition, a result of fifteen years as a professional dancer and a ski injury. Needless to say, I was not happy with the changes I saw in my face and body.

I began to question dermatologists, aestheticians, nutritionists, and other practitioners about what I might do to regenerate myself. The dermatologists gave me the least hope, telling me that once damage had occurred, it was too late to do anything short of plastic surgery. The aestheticians advised me to stay out of the sun and suggested products and salon treatments that would help improve my skin. The nutritionists were the most hopeful, telling me about vitamins and their restorative, healing effects on both the inside and outside of the body.

Following the aestheticians' advice, I decided to attempt to undo the damaging effects tanning had caused my skin. But first, in order to do this, I needed to understand what had caused it. As a result, my investigation taught me about the aging effects of ultraviolet light. So I began by allowing myself less sun exposure. This was the hardest thing for me because I loved being in the sun. After three years of tanning but not letting myself get *dark* tan, I saw some, but not enough, improvement. Thus I vowed to stay out of the sun completely and to protect my skin with a total sun block when I was exposed. Real improvement began. I watched my skin become less lined and more taut. In three years I saw the improvement I'd wanted; my face looked about 10 years younger than it had 6 years earlier!

Now, at the age of 43, it is not unusual for me to be taken for 15 years younger than I am. When my 22-year-old daughter and I go shopping together, salespeople assume that we're young friends. She loves calling me "Mother" to see their mouths drop open. When I do television and personal appearances, I dress and make up to look older. I'm afraid that if people see me the way I really look, they'll think I'm a kid and not take me seriously. When I was on tour with my book *Face Value: Skin Care for Women Over 35,* an indignant female reporter who assumed that she was a good deal older than me asked, "What do *you* know about skin care for older women?" She turned out to be 7 years younger than me.

My daughter Ari and me

Just as important is proper preparation for the cold, which is really no different from preparing to be in the sun; you need special clothing and skin protection for both. I cannot emphasize strongly enough the incredible difference you will see in your skin by simply protecting it from the damaging effects of the elements; this is the premier step in maintaining a youthful complexion, free of lines and wrinkles.

However, external maintenance is just part of the process of reprogramming yourself for extended youth. The mind also plays a large role. Fred Lehrman, director of Loving Relationships training and one of the first certified rebirthing therapists in this country, introduced me to another process for regenerating the body. This technique involves reprogramming the mind to heal the body. Fred, Sondra Ray, another rebirther and a Loving Relationships trainer and author, and several other "new age" people were experimenting with "youthing," a term they coined to define the opposite of aging.

Fred suggested that I choose an age at which I would like to keep my body. I decided that I'd like to keep it the way it looked in my mid-twenties. Now, I don't want to mislead you into thinking that this is solely a mental job. It is not. It takes exercise and good habits such as protecting the skin from ultraviolet light, eating well, and taking vitamins, as well as practicing good skin care. But our mental attitude is important because it *programs* and supports the body to make change possible. The mind creates the foundation for the body to build on. I've since adopted the term *youthing* to replace *aging*.

In recent years, research has finally proven the amount of power that the mind exerts over the body. Various scientific experiments, autosuggestion, hypnosis, and biofeedback techniques have had successful results in training people to steady uneven heart rates, reduce high blood pressure, and improve hearing. In a 1970 study in New Delhi, India, yoga practitioner Ramanand Yogi demonstrated the ability to slow his heart rate at will, decrease his intake of oxygen to one fourth of the minimum required for the maintenance of human life, and cause perspiration to appear at an isolated point on his body (the forehead). Modern psychology now accepts the fact that a person's mental state often affects and controls the physical state. If this is so, how may our minds be programming our bodies?

Dr. Robert Morgan, Dean for Academic and Professional Affairs at the California School of Professional Psychology and President of the Division of Gerontological Psychology for the International Association of Applied Psychology, regards the mind as a "dimension of the body rooted in the nervous system, not as something separate from the body. It is therefore important to the complete study of aging." Dr. Morgan defines aging as "a series of disadvantaging events that normally occur in our bodies over time. These events gradually reduce our ability to adapt to our surroundings in such a way that they increase the probability of death. The less efficient our bodies become, the more chances we have of dying." We may add years to our life-spans by reducing the number of "disadvantaging events" in our lives.

For example, let's look at one factor that very well may be the number one cause of aging: our belief systems—specifically the one that concentrates on how old we're getting. From early childhood we are exposed to the belief systems of those around us, and because of our naïveté, we are easily impressed by the beliefs that are held by those older whom we love and admire. As we grow up, these subliminally held beliefs begin to program our thinking, just as they programmed that of our elders.

I've designed a short quiz to give you an example of how this works. It may also help you uncover your subconscious beliefs on the subject of aging. Read the statements first to see if you associate them with specific elders from your childhood. Then reread them and check the ones that you've found *yourself* saying or thinking.

1. I guess I must be getting old.
2. That's just part of getting old.
3. I'm not getting any younger.
4. It's all downhill from here.
5. When I was young . . .
6. I'm not as young as I used to be.
7. When you're as old as I am . . .
8. Ever since I turned . . .

Reprogramming for Extended Youth

By the continued use and repetition of these and other litanies, are we actually programming ourselves to age? I believe that we are. Many teachers, researchers, and therapists also hold similar beliefs. Gerontologist Lawrence Casler refers to statements such as those listed above as "self-fulfilling prophecies." In an experiment with 30 residents of The Jewish Home and Hospital for the Aged, in New York City, he proved that these beliefs could be successfully manipulated.

The 30 people were divided into two groups; the experimental group was visited by Mr. Casler on a regular basis and given positive suggestions—

sometimes by hypnosis, sometimes just by conversation—regarding their health and vitality. The suggestions went something like this: "A person is as young as he feels. You may have many happy, healthy years ahead of you ... years full of opportunity for pursuing your interests and hobbies and developing new ones, making new friends, and enjoying life free of financial and other responsibilities. You will find it easy to relax, to enjoy yourself, and to remain healthy and happy for many years to come." The control group received no visits or suggestions of any kind, but were left to their normal, everyday routine.

Mr. Casler followed up on his experimental and control groups one year after the sessions had ended and found that the experimental group had less sickness and fewer injuries and hospitalizations than the control group. Their rate of recovery was also markedly faster. Of the control group, six of the original fifteen had died within the year, while only one of the experimental group had died. In the years that followed, the experimental group lived more than four times as long as the control group.

Using a slightly different technique, Leonard Elkind, a clinical psychologist and hypnotherapist in San Francisco, illustrated the impact of hypnosis on aging. He developed tests designed to measure the various effects of aging on different parts of the body. In these experiments he used women between the ages of 39 and 53, and implanted positive thoughts regarding youth and vitality. Within four weeks, one session reduced the subjects' "body age" (as measured by his methods of testing) by an average of 11 years.

Mr. Elkind describes hypnosis as a "technique that speaks to the part of the mind that regulates the body," and believes it to be the most powerful tool capable of intervening in the aging process. This does not mean that you need to begin extensive hypnotherapy treatment. In fact, Mr. Elkind states that all hypnosis is self-hypnosis and the therapist merely "helps to put his subject into a better hypnotic state." There are other practitioners who share similar beliefs and have developed various types of self-help treatments based on theories such as these. Just a few of the most popular books on this subject are *The Answer Within: A Clinical Framework of Ericksonian Hypnotherapy,* by Stephen R. Lankton and Carol H. Lankton (Brunner-Mazel, 1983); *Hypnotherapy: An Exploratory Case Book,* by Milton H. Erickson (Ervington, 1979); *The Nature of Hypnosis and Suggestion,* by Dr. Milton H. Erickson (Ervington, 1980); *Love Is Letting Go of Fear,* by Dr. Gerald Jampolsky (Celestial Arts, 1979); *Creative Visualization,* by Shakti Gawain (Bantam, 1985); *Mind as Healer, Mind as Slayer,* by Kenneth Pelleltier (Dell, 1977); *Pulling Your Own Strings,* by Dr. Wayne Dyer (Avon, 1979); *The Owners Manual for Your Life,* by Stewart Emmery and Neal Rogin (Pocket Books, 1984); and *Inner Joy,* by Dr. Harold Bloomfield (Jove, 1985).

If you are under the age of 30, you're at an even greater advantage because you haven't reached the point of thinking of yourself as old. Regardless of age, I believe that you are as old or as young as you feel. The choice is yours. I would like to ask you to stretch your imagination a bit and play a little game with yourself. Pretend that it is possible to turn back the clock. Consciously make a decision to stop saying and thinking aging phrases and replace them with positive statements such as, "I feel great at [whatever age you are]," or "Life keeps getting better." Notice the changes in your mental attitude after just a week or two of this. If you see even a small improvement, take it one step further and decide what you'd like to change or improve about your body. Try some of the practices and suggestions in this book, but don't give up if you don't see drastic improvements in a week or two. Remember that it took years for your skin and body to develop the signs of age you notice and it will take time to reverse the aging process. Many of the treatments I recommend begin to take effect after a period of 1 to 3 months. It may even take 2 to 3 years for you to see the end results of the improvements you've envisioned. Program yourself for success and give whatever you choose to try a realistic chance to work. Track your progress on a weekly or bimonthly basis, rather than daily. I'm currently working on a 2- to 3-year program to improve the sun-damaged skin on my body. The thought of looking younger in coming years is very appealing to me. After all, the years are going to go by anyway. Why not make them work *for* you?

How Stress Affects Aging

Another example of how the mind affects the body may be seen in the area of stress. Traditionally stress was blamed for maladies such as ulcers, psoriasis, ileitis, and colitis; now researchers believe that stress, of all types, may be one of the major causes of aging. How stress affects the body, along with anti-stress techniques, has become a favorite subject of major magazines.

It is not merely the stressful occurrence that affects us, it is our *perception* of it. For example, when an argument or upsetting event occurs, a negative image travels from the midbrain's outer layer (cortex) toward the center, where the hypothalamus is located. The hypothalamus is similar to a dispatching station; it receives the negative image and sends out warnings to its entire territory of organs and glands. The production of adrenaline is one result. Hormonal secretions, which reduce the efficacy of white blood cells, are also activated. White blood cells are an integral part of our body's immune system, and when they are impaired, the body is left open to infection. This helps us understand the connection between stress and illness.

Worry, which generally follows a stressful occurrence, perpetuates the stress effect. How you deal with the *aftermath* of a stressful situation is what really determines the effect that situation has on your body. Learning how to mentally counter these effects can add years to your life and make daily living more pleasant. This can result in an improvement in the appearance of the body itself. When you feel emotionally better, your body functions better and ultimately looks better.

I am not suggesting that you totally avoid stressful situations. That's impossible. But you can prepare your body and mind for these types of situations in advance so that you are able to protect yourself from their negative effects. If all you can do is shorten the amount of time you feel stress, you will have accomplished a lot.

Let's examine the extent to which a stressful situation can affect you. Let's say that one morning a disagreement occurs between you and a fellow worker and does not get resolved during the day. It's highly possible that you will be upset throughout the day. Will you be able to leave those feelings when you leave work or will they go home with you? Chances are you'll take the upset home and by that time, after hours of stress, additional physiological changes will have occurred. As a result of stress, the level of endorphins, the body's natural tranquilizers, falls. This may cause nervousness, tiredness, and depression. In addition, in an effort to make you feel better, the body releases pain-relieving substances that interfere with intestinal secretions necessary for digestion. For this reason, stress is often associated with indigestion. Improper digestion and assimilation of food lead to constipation, bloating, and facial breakouts. To make matters worse, stress produces a rise in the blood level of free fatty acids. These are organic acids that combine with glycerin to form fat, thus explaining the rise in blood cholesterol levels during stressful periods. Triglycerides, the type of fat stored by the body and linked to heart disease, also increase by as much as 50 percent. All of these changes drastically affect your body, your thought processes, and the way you relate to others.

Needless to say, it is difficult and sometimes impossible to get a good night's sleep when you are under stress. That, in turn, affects the way you greet the next day. Few people can miss sleep and still look attractive. Bags under the eyes, a sallow complexion, and a tired appearance are all characteristic of too little sleep. It's now 24 hours later and one occurrence has had a tremendously negative mental and physical effect on you. If the matter remains unresolved, *even if only in your mind,* for any length of time, it could have a serious effect on your well-being. Now, consider the fact that it is not unusual for this type of altercation to be repeated many times during the course of one day. Without some type of anti-stress technique, stress can eventually do irreparable harm.

Everyday Anti-stress Techniques

You can significantly reduce the effects of stress in your life by one or more of the anti-stress techniques discussed here.

Exercise must be a part of your weekly routine. Ideally, it should be part of your daily routine. You may do anything from brisk walking to a strenuous aerobics class. Depending on whether you have any individual restrictions (which you should discuss first with your doctor), you can alternate between several different types of exercises—bicycling one day, taking a dance class one day, playing racquetball or taking a swim the next. You can even jump rope in your living room. It doesn't matter what you do as long as it raises your heart rate for approximately 20 minutes. This is known as an aerobic anti-stress method. The increased oxygen and rise in body temperature cause the body to produce beta-endorphins, hormonal secretions that make us feel good and suppress the appetite. The same substances are produced when we experience the emotional feeling of being in love. Another benefit of aerobic exercise is that it prompts the body to produce collagen, resulting in younger-looking skin. It also helps to stimulate the oil and sweat glands to produce the lubricants that keep the skin moist.

An alternative type of exercise is non-aerobic. Yoga is the best example. It is based on the premise that vital energy that is stored in the body may be released and used to overcome deterioration of the body and mind. The slow, stretching movements tone muscles, while the accompanying breathing brings oxygen to the blood and soothes the psyche. Because it teaches relaxation, yoga is an excellent form of exercise for people who find it hard to relax. Its gentleness and slowness make it ideal for older people whose movements may be impaired. If you don't have time for a yoga class, there are several yoga videotapes on the market, including one by Raquel Welch that is excellent.

Another excellent gentle exercise program is Callanetics. Introduced by Callan Pinckney in her book *Callanetics: Ten Years Younger in Ten Hours* (Morrow, 1984), it combines slow, isometric exercises with basic yoga and dance stretches to create one of the most effective body sculpting programs I've ever found. It is an excellent anti-stress technique as well and a nice alternative to aerobics classes, loud music, screaming instructors, and jarring movements. Callanetics is also available as a 60-minute video, which makes the instruction easier to follow.

Here are some other guidelines for stress management:

Don't forget to breathe. This may sound silly, but stress affects our breathing and, consequently, our supply of oxygen. Our bodies need oxygen to build new skin cells. Skin that is deprived of oxygen is sallow or gray and appears lifeless. Take time during the day to inhale and exhale several deep breaths, slowly, through your nose. This may be done anywhere you feel comfortable; at home, in the office, while driving or riding on public transportation. For more specific information you may want to read *The Art of Breathing: Thirty Simple Exercises for Improving Your Performance and Well-Being,* by Nancy Zi (Bantam, 1986).

Beware of stress-causing substances such as caffeine, tobacco, and white sugar. They rob the body of vitamins A, B complex, E, and C, oxygen, minerals, and trace elements, which are necessary to maintain body/mind balance. Caffeine and tobacco also cause the constriction of blood vessels and capillaries which carry nutrients to the cells. When they are constricted, fewer nutrients, if any, get through, and without these nutrients the body is unable to build and repair cells.

Consider supplementing your diet with anti-stress nutrients:

Vitamin B complex: 100–200 mg daily (sample dosage only)

Calcium: 3,000 mg daily (two times a day and before bed) (sample dosage only)

Discuss specific dosages and your individual needs with your doctor or nutritionist.

Learn to meditate, even if only for a few minutes each day. Meditation calms your mind and relaxes your body. This quiet state of being is not only relaxing, it is very easy to let go of disturbing thoughts and replace them with positive ones. You might find it interesting to browse through the metaphysics section of your local library or book store and choose a book on the subject of meditation. There are hundreds of books to choose from, dealing with dozens of different styles of meditative teachings. It is difficult for me to recommend a particular style, because even though it may be effective, it may not be right for you.

How to Reprogram Yourself for Extended Youth

Stan Russell is a 62-year-old human potential researcher and teacher who lives in Sausalito, California. A feature film producer and marketing executive, Stan has spent the past 35 years of his life in pursuit of knowledge aimed at the improvement of the human body, mind, and spirit. He has also lectured on and taught tantric yoga, Hawaiian Huna, Neuro Linguistic Programming, Ericksonian hypnosis, and personal marketing, to name a few. When meeting Stan, it is obvious that he is a product of his own teachings; he looks 15 years younger than his age and possesses the unusual ability to establish an immediate, almost intimate rapport with others.

Stan has found that most people who are intent on changing their behavior need to develop a rapport with their "inner self." He observes that rapport is necessary in order for communication to take place. The first step in communicating with your inner self, then, is to develop a rapport with it. This means accepting it as it is, and acknowledging and appreciating it. Only then can you successfully program it, or "reframe" it. Stan describes reframing as a process of replacing old, destructive, negative habits and patterns with new, constructive, positive ones.

Stan believes that regardless of your age it is possible to "slow down the biological clock," as well as expand your physical and mental abilities. I would like to pass on to you his following advice:

Step 1: In short, simple sentences, write out a one-page list of the rewards and consequences that you will experience when you have developed the new pattern of behavior that you desire. In other words, state specifically how your life will be improved or what you will have when the change you desire is produced. For example, if you wish to look and feel ten years younger, describe what that will mean to your life. You may say something like, "People find me attractive," "I have as much energy as I need," "My body is firm and strong," or "I love the way I look." Be sure to construct only positive sentences.

Keep the page of sentences next to your bed and read them every morning before getting out of bed. This will motivate you, and if you are not motivated, you won't do what is necessary to accomplish your goals.

Step 2: Take one step at a time. It can become overwhelming to look at everything you have to do at once. The truth is that nothing is done "all at once."

Step 3: Acknowledge yourself for each little thing you do along the way to your goal. Allow yourself to feel satisfaction. There is no need to withhold satisfaction until the end result is achieved.

Step 4: Take a few minutes each day to daydream or visualize yourself having completed your goal. Feel the sensations and have a full, sensory experience of what you are moving toward. Allow yourself to mentally enjoy the benefits of having reached your goal.

Step 5: It's helpful to have some support. You may want to get together with a friend to facilitate each other toward your goal. This is also a good way to share acknowledgment.

Step 6: Have a model who inspires you. It doesn't matter who this person is, as long as you have a clear picture of him or her. You may even want to post an actual photograph of your model somewhere in your home.

Step 7: Recognize that the part of you from which behavior emanates is very conservative and changes slowly. The way human beings change may be compared to the way that plants grow; each small step leads to the next until significant growth is complete and visible. Change cannot be forced or happen all at once. If you attempt instant, radical change, you will be setting yourself up for more stress and possible disappointment.

Step 8: Realize that the characteristic that you want to change has served you in some way. If you change it abruptly, you will become unstable or disoriented. Confusion, uncertainty, doubt, and anxiety are all characteristics of rapid growth. When these occur, there is a temptation to grab on to something familiar, which could be the old characteristic. If you recognize that these things are related to the growth process, you can avoid responding to them.

These eight suggestions will help you lay the framework for lasting change to take place. Use your mind to alter the *cause* of negative thoughts, the results of which show up on your body. The specific techniques discussed throughout the rest of the book will help you to reduce or rid yourself of the *results* of negative thoughts on your body.

CHAPTER
TWO

EATING FOR A
YOUTHFUL BODY

There is no doubt that diet is a major concern of the American people, who for the past 5 years have made diet books consistent best sellers. There also can be no doubt as to what people want from these diets; health is not the primary concern, thinness is. Even health-oriented diet books, such as *The Pritikin Program for Diet and Exercise* (Bantam, 1980), offer thinness as an added benefit to good health.

In the 1980s, exercise has been the subject of many best-selling videotapes. Although cardiovascular fitness is one of the aims of aerobic exercise, again, health is not the motivational force behind these videos; a thin, shapely body is. However, the American medical community agrees: A thin person stands a greater chance of being healthy than does a fat person.

Regardless of motivation, both diet and exercise trends have proven to be healthy for Americans. During the past several years, many divergent schools of thought have emerged. Several years ago a high-protein diet was considered good for supplying energy and burning excess fat. Then it was discovered that most Americans consume more protein than they need. If the protein consumed came from an animal source, it meant high cholesterol, which was bad for the blood and heart. Liquid protein diets, which avoided the pitfalls of animal protein, were responsible for several deaths due to their inability to supply other necessary nutrients, specifically selenium and potassium.

Fruit-based diets have always been popular with those people interested in quick weight loss and inner cleansing of the body. But staying on a fruit-only diet for too long causes protein deprivation that leads to hair loss, headaches, physical and mental weakness, more serious maladies, and sometimes death. The high-carbohydrate diet became popular a few years ago and was welcomed with particular enthusiasm by those who had been denying themselves foods such as pasta and potatoes on other diets.

Diets with longevity in mind, as opposed to those merely concerned with weight loss, have brought attention to the existence of "free radicals" —chemical substances with unpaired electrons. Free radicals result partially from normal metabolism but are greatly increased by the ingestion of chemicals, cigarette smoke, alcohol, and the exposure to ultraviolet light, smog, and pollution. Their "free" or unpaired state drives them to attach themselves to something in an attempt to pair up their free electrons. When they join onto cells, oxidation occurs. And oxidation is responsible for the breakdown of cells that precedes aging and disease. Denham Harman, M.D., Ph.D., of the University of Nebraska College of Medicine, is acknowledged as the "father" of the free radical theory. He discovered their existence during longevity experiments with rodents. To counteract the effect of free radicals, Dr. Harman fed the test animals a diet high in the antioxidant preservatives BHT and MEA. These two preservatives fight oxidation in cells, which causes cellular breakdown and leads to illness and aging. As a result, he was able to extend the animals' life-spans by as much as 29 percent. However, I do not recommend ingesting a diet high in artificial preservatives. For human beings, there is a much healthier way to accomplish greater longevity by the use of vitamin supplements.

Vitamin Supplements

Certain vitamins are powerful antioxidants that fight or neutralize free radicals. These same vitamins have been touted by nutritionists and "health nuts" for years as being useful for prolonging the sex drive, increasing energy, protecting against sickness, and preventing cancer and arteriosclerosis. Although researchers disagree on the recommended daily amounts of these 11 nutrients, all concur on their importance as anti-aging, free radical chasers. They also boost each other's effectiveness when taken together. I studied the recommended daily amounts given by several nutritionists. The amounts given here are an average of their recommendations and should be taken daily, with meals. But before beginning any vitamin program, it is advisable to check with your doctor or nutritionist, to be sure that the specific supplements and daily amounts are right for you.

ANTI-AGING NUTRIENTS

Nutrient	*Average Daily Amounts*
1) Vitamin A	25,000 IU
2) Vitamin B_1	100 mg
3) Vitamin B_2	100 mg
4) Vitamin B_3	250 mg–3 grams
5) Vitamin B_5	400 mg
6) Vitamin B_6	100 mg
7) Vitamin B_{12}	100 mg
8) Vitamin C	1–2 grams
9) Vitamin E	600–800 IU
10) Vitamin D	400 IU
11) Zinc	15–30 mg

The following foods are excellent sources of these antioxidant vitamins:

Vitamin A: carrots, sweet potatoes, cantaloupe, broccoli, and spinach

Vitamin B complex: nuts, seeds, dried beans, brown rice, wheat germ, brewers' yeast, bran, oats, eggs, tuna, mushrooms, broccoli, dark green vegetables, chicken, bananas, yogurt, potatoes, and sprouts

Vitamin C: citrus fruits, green pepper, papaya, brussel sprouts, broccoli, and cantaloupe

Vitamin D is manufactured by the body when it is exposed to sunlight. The average person needs approximately 20 minutes of daily exposure in the winter and 10 minutes in the summer. Remember to protect your skin with a sun block whenever it is exposed to the sun. This will not hamper vitamin D production in any way.

Vitamin E: wheat germ oil, raw wheat germ, almonds, pecans, hazelnuts, sunflower seeds, and sunflower seed oil

Zinc: dairy products, fish, chicken, sunflower seeds, whole grains, and mushrooms

The more you increase your intake of these important nutrients through food, the less supplements you'll need to take. However, it is important to remember that fresh foods begin to lose their nutritional value within 24 hours after being harvested. Foods that have been refrigerated also quickly lose their value. It is almost impossible to determine the nutritional value of store-bought produce, unless you buy from a local farm stand or grower where produce is harvested daily. It is for this reason that I recommend taking supplements.

Don't Crash Diet...
Eat Right All the Time

There seem to be four motivating reasons for people to go on a diet: weight loss, health, longevity, and the desire to improve the appearance of their bodies. Unfortunately, if the chosen diet is not sensible and varied enough to become a permanent way of eating, its benefits will be short-lived. The weight-return rate following crash diets is about 90 percent.

A sensible way of eating all the time, rather than sporadic dieting, will help you to accomplish all four of the dieter's goals. Good eating habits also become effortless and interesting with time, rather than tedious and boring. The more you learn about incorporating beneficial eating habits into your everyday life, the more choices become available to you.

There is no one diet that I can recommend to you for a beautiful, young body. Instead, I would like to give you the information you need to begin discovering a healthy, creative way to eat. Since every body is unique and has different needs, you need to become the expert on your own body. This will ultimately allow you to have the body you want, and to live a longer life while enjoying excellent health.

How to Eliminate Substances that
Accelerate Aging from Your Diet

The first thing you need to know is that certain substances will cause your body to age by depleting it of necessary nutrients. These substances are caffeine, artificial colorings and flavorings, nitrates, nitrites, aspirin, estrogen drugs, recreational drugs, antibiotics, and birth control pills. There are other substances responsible for nutritional depletion that age you by causing oxidation in your cells. The abuse of these substances—salt, sugar, saturated fats and cholesterol, alcohol, nicotine, toxins such as pesticides, and mercury—may also eventually kill you. Let's look at each of the most dangerous substances individually.

Salt is consumed by the average American adult in a quantity measured at approximately 40 times more than necessary. For good health, our bodies require about .25 gram of salt a day, as opposed to the 10 grams consumed by most Americans. Excess salt contributes to high blood pressure, which puts a terrible strain on the body and can eventually cause it to break down permanently. Salt is also responsible for water retention, which causes bloating and accentuates cellulite.

The most obvious way to cut down on the amount of salt in your diet is to stop adding it to your food. You will be surprised at how sensitive you become to the taste of salt after just a few weeks without it. Replace canned and prepared frozen foods with fresh foods. Almost all canned and frozen foods contain high amounts of salt. If you like canned tuna or salmon, drain it into a strainer and rinse well under cold, running water to wash off the sodium/water solution in which it is packed.

There are hundreds of salt-free foods available at your local supermarket. Substitute salt-free crackers such as Wasa bread for commercial crackers. If you crave potato chips, popcorn, or similar snack foods, buy the salt-free ones. Be aware of the fact that all luncheon meats and hot dogs are made with salt. Replace them with freshly cooked turkey, roast beef, or chicken. All ham and bacon are prepared with salt. Look for hidden salt in foods such as peanut butter, mustard, catsup, mayonnaise, pickles, relish, and bread.

When cooking, substitute herbs and spices for salt. These may also be added to cooked foods for additional seasoning. Most health food stores offer several brands of ready-mixed herbs for this purpose. Take a good look at the foods you normally eat and you'll be amazed at the amount of salt they contain.

I do not recommend salt substitutes such as Lite, because they are not salt-free, but only lower in sodium than regular table salt. Read labels and learn about the foods you may never have questioned before. When you begin to take responsibility for what you put into your body, you will find it very easy to eliminate those things that you know are detrimental.

Sugar may not yet be acknowledged by the major portion of the medical community as being lethal, but recent studies conducted at the United States Drug Administration's Human Nutrition Information Service have proven that sugar raises serum cholesterol, triglyceride, and insulin levels in adults.

Eliminate or cut down on the amount of refined sugar in your diet. If you are a heavy consumer, this may not be easy, as sugar is an addictive substance. You may want to read the book *Sugar Blues,* by William Dufty (Warner, 1976), for inspiration and insight into sugar addiction. Substitute fresh fruit, raisins, dried dates, figs, apricots, or even natural, sugarless chewing gum when you have a sweet craving. Use honey in place of sugar for baking and in preserves. Because it is twice as sweet as sugar, you will only need to use half as much, which also helps to save on calories. Honey is also delicious as a sweetener for decaffeinated coffee or tea. I do not, however, recommend artificial sweeteners such as saccharin or aspartame for use in hot beverages because they have been shown to cause cancer in laboratory animals.

Saturated fats and cholesterol can cause heart attacks and arteriosclerosis. Very simply, the hardened fat clogs veins, making the passage of blood difficult and eventually impossible. This type of fat is also stored by the body to form the fat that we see.

Animal fat is the highest source of saturated fats and cholesterol. Limiting your intake of dairy products is one of the easiest ways to cut down on this type of fat. If you like milk, use low-fat or nonfat instead of whole. Choose low-fat cottage cheese, nonfat yogurt, sour half and half instead of sour cream, and whipped cream cheese instead of regular. Cut down on the amount of cheese in your diet and try low-salt/low-fat cheeses or soya instead. Use a safflower oil mayonnaise substitute instead of those made with eggs and try low-fat frozen yogurt in place of ice cream. As a rule, I do not recommend dairy substitutes such as Mocha Mix because of the high quantity of artificial ingredients in them. Margarine is another questionable substitute because it is high in polyunsaturated fats, which are believed to contribute to high blood cholesterol levels. Whenever possible, use cold-pressed vegetable oils in place of either butter or margarine. Egg consumption should be kept to a minimum—one or two a week, instead of one or two a day. Limit the amount of red meat you eat, choose lean cuts over fatty ones, and trim the excess fat before cooking. Choose low-fat meats such as poultry, veal, and lamb over pork and beef, removing the fat and poultry skin before cooking. I've substituted ground chicken or turkey for ground beef in recipes from hamburgers to meat balls with great success. If the market where you shop doesn't offer ground chicken or turkey, ask the butcher to remove all fat and skin and grind it especially for you. Eating fish in place of meat is an excellent idea for more reasons than cutting down on fat. Fish supplies natural oils, and is high in vitamin A, a potent antioxidant and nutrient, as well as Omega-3 fatty acids, which benefit the cardiovascular system and discourage the formation of cholesterol.

If you're used to frying or sautéeing fish or poultry, try broiling or poaching it instead. If you're concerned with your weight, poach in water with herbs, garlic, shallots, or onions. If calories are not important to you, use wine or part wine and part water. The poaching liquid may then be reduced (cooked down) to make a light sauce. This type of cooking eliminates fats, oils, and flour, but tastes delicious. Almost all the new cookbooks give interesting poaching recipes for fish and fowl.

Alcohol and nicotine are major causes of oxidation in cells. They also cause constriction of blood vessels that carry nutrients and oxygen to cells. They dehydrate the body and rob it of the vitamins, trace elements, and minerals necessary for it to function properly.

Light to moderate alcohol consumption is considered acceptable by most doctors and nutritionists. In fact, many recommend a daily glass or two of red wine as being healthy; some believe it helps to build red blood cells. Wine is also high in chromium, one of the elements that fights heart disease. Beer is even more acceptable because of its low alcohol content. Light beers are a good choice because they have fewer calories as well as less alcohol. One or two ounces of hard liquor daily, such as scotch or vodka, is also considered acceptable, but for some people this is too much. Regardless of what the norm may be, getting to know what works best for *you* is the key.

If you are going to drink at all, it is important to replace the nutrients that will be lost. On an evening when you've had a drink or two, consider taking the following vitamins with a spoonful of yogurt and a large glass of water before going to bed, and again the next morning with breakfast: an average dose would be vitamin E, 800 IU; vitamin C, 100 mg; vitamin B complex, 100 mg; and calcium/magnesium, 1,000 mg/250 mg.

You may also want to try a dosage of 500 mg. Evening Primrose oil, which contains an unusually high amount (8%) of "GLA" (gamma linoleic acid). GLA helps the body to maintain its natural prostaglanoin (an essential cellular hormone) levels, which are lowered by the consumption of alcohol.

Pesticides, mercury, and other toxins remain in the body and cause oxidation in cells. This may later lead to the development of cancer. To thoroughly remove toxins from the skins of vegetables and fruits, soak them for 10 minutes in a large bowl of water to which you have added a few drops of liquid Clorox, no more than 2-3 drops from an eye dropper, then rinse again in clean, running, water. If you live in an area with a reliable health food store or produce stand, you will be able to buy organically raised produce. This is usually more expensive than commercially raised produce but tastes so much better that it is worth the extra cost.

It is impossible for most people to totally avoid the aforementioned substances. If you can manage to avoid most and aim for moderation in others, you will certainly improve your body and lengthen your life-span.

Feed Your Body—
The Anti-Aging Way

Now that you know what to avoid and how to make healthy substitutions, I'd like to tell you about foods that help your body to function at its peak and fight the breakdowns that are associated with age and illness.

Fiber is one of the most important cleansers of the body. It passes through your digestive tract unabsorbed, taking with it undigested waste that can otherwise impede digestion and poison your body. The more effectively your body processes what you eat, the fewer problems you will have. The faster food moves through your intestines, the less time there is for fat and cholesterol to be absorbed by your body. Research has proven, over and over again, that a high-fiber diet is one of the best preventives against heart disease; arteriosclerosis; intestinal, breast, and colon cancer; diabetes; hemorrhoids; and constipation. Fiber also slows the absorption of sugar, helping to regulate blood insulin levels.

There are two main types of fiber: pectin, found primarily in fruits and vegetables, and cellulose, found predominantly in whole grains such as oats and wheat, and especially in bran, the broken coat of grain seeds. Pectin helps break up cholesterol in the blood and cellulose aids the passage of foods through the intestines.

Some good sources of fiber are raw bran, oats, whole wheat cereals and breads, wheat berries, dry beans and peas, raw apples, raw carrots, almonds, spinach, broccoli, cabbage, and celery.

Complex carbohydrates, such as rice, nuts, pasta, breads, seeds, fresh fruits, and vegetables, also supply fiber along with energy. Carbohydrates make an excellent diet staple because they burn slowly and do not contain fat.

Protein is one of the body's most important building blocks. But the average American diet relies too heavily on animal protein, which is high in saturated fat and cholesterol, as well as the growth hormones, antibiotics, and pesticides contained in commercial feeds. Fish, low-fat dairy products, dried beans, tofu, nuts, seeds, and grains supply excellent low-fat protein.

I hope that I have piqued your interest in the area of nutrition, although I have merely scratched the surface of the subject. It is a fascinating one that can make an enormous difference in the quality and length of your life. If you wish to learn more, there are dozens of books available that you may find interesting and inspiring. Some of my favorites are:

The Complete Guide to Anti-Aging Nutrients, by Sheldon S. Hendler, M.D., Ph.D. Simon and Schuster, 1985
Diet For A Small Planet, by Frances Moore Lappét. Ballantine, 1982
Growing Younger: How to Add Years to Your Life by Measuring and Controlling Your Body Age, by Dr. Robert F. Morgan with Jane Wilson. Stein and Day, 1983
In Pursuit of Youth: Everyday Nutrition for Everyone over 35, by Betty and Si Kamen. Dodd Mead, 1984

Life Extension: Adding Years to Your Life and Life to Your Years: A Practical Scientific Approach, by Durk Pearson and Sandy Shaw. Warner, 1982

The Life Extension Weight Loss Program, by Durk Pearson and Sandy Shaw. Doubleday, 1986

The Life-Extension Revolution: The Definitive Guide to Better Health, Longer Life, and Physical Immortality, by Saul Kent. Morrow, 1980

Mega-Nutrition: The New Prescription for Maximum Health, Energy and Longevity, by Richard A. Kunin, M.D. New American Library, 1981

Nutrition Against Aging, by Michael A. Weiner, Ph.D., and Kathleen Goss. Bantam Books, 1983

The Practical Encyclopedia of Natural Healing, by Mark Bricklin. Rodale, 1983

Sugar Blues, by William Dufty. Warner, 1976

Women Coming of Age, by Jane Fonda and Mignon McCarthy. Simon and Schuster, 1984

C H A P T E R
THREE

BODY SKIN

From head to toe, the skin on the body varies in thickness and degree of sensitivity. For this reason, different areas require different types of care. In this chapter I will discuss basic body care and general treatments. The hands, feet, neck, and throat will be discussed separately in other chapters.

Caring for facial skin can be a very complex issue. However, there are some general points you should know: First, you must determine your skin type before you can institute a program of proper skin care. Second, the skin on the face differs from the skin on the rest of the body because of its thinness, sensitivity, underlying muscular and vascular structures, and continual exposure to the elements. You may have noticed that certain creams or lotions that you use on your body cannot be used on your face. You may have also "tested" a particular cosmetic for allergy or sensitivity on the inside of your arm and gotten no adverse reaction, only to find that when used on your face it made you break out. Third, the wide range of cosmetics designed for use on the face, such as cleansers, toners, moisturizers, masks, cellular recovery creams, and various types of makeup, requires dozens of pages of in-depth explanations regarding composition, application, and usage. Although this may sound complicated, actually caring for your face is not a complicated process; in fact, it takes only about 3 minutes twice a day. The key to any effective skin care program is learning what is right *for you.* For these reasons I strongly suggest that you familiarize yourself with the workings of the facial skin by reading one of my books that treat this subject more thoroughly. I have written two books for women on the care of facial skin—*Putting on Your Face: The*

Ultimate Guide to Cosmetics, (Bantam, 1985), and *Face Value: Skin Care for Women Over 35,* (Bantam, 1986)—and one for men—*Skin Care for Men Only: A Complete Guide,* (Harcourt Brace Jovanovich, 1987).

Daily Care

The average American adult bathes once a day. The average American adult who participates in an exercise routine bathes twice a day. If soap is used all over the body on a regular basis, the result will be dry skin. In their quest for cleanliness, most Americans bathe too much and use too much soap.

Soap works by surrounding dirt, oil, and sweat so that it may be carried from the surface of the skin. But soap cannot discern between a normal amount of natural oils and an excess of other substances. Consequently, it also surrounds and washes away the body's natural surface oils. If a person with any type of skin other than oily washes with soap and water once or twice a day, the body may not have enough time to replenish its natural lubricants between washings. This results in dry skin, itchiness, redness, sensitivity, a scaly appearance to the skin, dandruff, keratosis pilaris, and premature aging.

To avoid drying your skin out unnecessarily, use soap only where it is needed. Most people taking a morning shower need to use soap only under the arms and between the legs. Only those with oily skin may need to use soap on the chest and back. Unless your body skin has actually become dirty or sweaty from working out or from some other type of hard work, it is not necessary to use soap.

The type of soap you use makes a big difference in the amount of dryness it may cause. Ivory soap and deodorant soaps leave a film on the surface of the skin and are the most drying. For this reason I never recommend them. Glycerine soaps, or those containing emollients, are the least drying types. These may be found in health food stores, department stores, and bath shops. Caswell-Massey's Almond Soap is one of my favorites. Dove soap is the most emollient of the commercial brands, but it is not hard-milled and becomes soft and mushy after one or two uses. Doak Pharmacal makes a good soap called Formula 405 Moisturizing Fragrance-free Soap. Pierre Cattier soaps are made in France of natural ingredients and sold here in health food stores. There are five different types for various types of skin, such as sensitive, dry, and oily. Soaps made from pure olive oil are another excellent choice and are easy to find in health food stores or cosmetic/bath shops.

The products I recommend are sold in various types of stores, which I have abbreviated in the following way throughout the text:

Department store = DS   Facial salon   = S
Health food store = H   Mail Order   = M
Pharmacy   = P

SOAPS

Caswell-Massey's Almond Soap	M
Formula 405 Moisturizing Fragrance-free Soap	P
Pierre Cattier's Nature de France soaps	H

If you are sensitive or allergic to soap, you may want to try a "soapless soap." These contain no animal fat (tallow) or lye and are sold in pharmacies.

SOAPLESS SOAPS

AveenoBar	P
Eucerin	P
Lowila	P

If you would rather not use soap at all, there are several liquid body cleansers that may be used instead. Most of these have a base of the synthetic detergent sodium laurel sulfate, which, although it dissolves the body's natural oils, does not leave a drying film on the skin. Many of these cleansers are made in Europe. The most famous one is Vitabath Shower Gelée ,which is sold in department stores and pharmacies. Paul Penders Natural Herbal Shower Gel is sold in health food stores. Annemarie Borlind Body Wash Lotion contains herbal extracts with antiseptic and disinfecting properties. These help to make it the only natural deodorant cleanser presently available. Borlind products are sold in health food stores and facial salons. When using any of these, or any cleanser, it is important to rinse well so that no detergent is left on the skin. If you have very sensitive skin and would rather not use even a gentle detergent, try Aqualin's Cleanser which is available in health food stores or by mail order: 1-800-626-7888.

Taking a long, hot bath is one of the easiest ways to relax at home. Few things are as convenient and inexpensive. However, few things are as dehydrating. This need not be the case. There are several things you can do to make your bath beneficial to your skin as well as relaxing.

1. **Don't** make the bath water very, very hot. The hotter the water, the more dehydrating it will be. Extremely hot water can also break capillaries, especially on the chest area, which is prone to this.
2. **Do** add bath oil to the water. This will help to make it less dehydrating. I prefer natural, vegetable bath oils over mineral oil based ones because they contain valuable nutrients such as vitamins E and A. They also mix more readily with water. Mineral oil-based products float on the surface of the bath water and are of no benefit to the skin.

   Natural, vegetable bath oils are not sold in drug stores with the exception of one, Neutrogena Body Oil. This has a base of sesame oil and although it is designed primarily for use after bathing, it may also be added to bath water. Some other good natural ones are Paul Penders Creamy Bath Oil and Sunshine Glowing Touch Skin Care Oil. Natural oils are available in health food stores and specialty bath shops.

   The Weleda Company makes three different bath oils based on the healing art of aromatherapy (discussed at length in Chapter 4). Each is designed to have a different effect on the body. They contain high concentrations of medicinal herbs in a sulfated castor oil base. The sulfated base helps to disperse the oil in water. The Rosemary Bath Oil is invigorating, although the scent is very medicinal. Lavender Bath Oil is soothing. Because it is deeply relaxing, Pine Needle Bath Oil is designed for late-night bathing. Taking a bath in this type of oil is very different from other types of baths. Unlike ordinary perfumes, the herbs have a powerful effect on the body. The only other type of bath products as strong as these are seaweed and nutritional additives, which I will discuss in Chapter 4.

   Weleda products can be bought in health food stores.
3. **Don't** soak for more than 10 minutes in an oil bath unless it is of the aromatherapy type. Since there is no real value in a plain bath oil, the relaxation will come from being submerged in hot water. The addition of the oil is merely to make the soak less dehydrating.
4. **Do** use a bath pillow to support your neck and make relaxation more complete. These are sold in bath shops, pharmacies, and department stores. If you find it difficult to simply lie still in a tub, try reading. The bath pillow will make this easy to do.
5. **Don't** use bubble bath or foaming bath gels. These contain sudsing agents, such as sodium laurel sulfate, which dissolve the skin's natural oils. They may also leave a layer on the skin, similar to that left by soap, if they are not rinsed off.
6. **Do** use a natural mineral salt such as Zia Cosmetic's Sea Soak, which

contains Dead Sea salts and plant extracts to remineralize the skin and soothe tired, aching muscles.

7. **Do** apply a body oil or lotion to damp skin directly following a bath. This helps to seal in moisture and prevent dryness. Body oils are better because of their ability to penetrate. Choose one that is water soluble, like Neutrogena Body Oil or Weleda Citrus Body Oil. An excellent selection of this type of body oil is made by Bare Escentuals, a small company in Los Gatos, California. Their base is jojoba oil, which closely resembles the oil produced by the human body and has an excellent ability to penetrate the skin. Another nice thing about buying these particular oils is that the company will design their fragrance according to your personal taste. You may choose from dozens of natural, essential oils, to make your own, unique combinations. If you are interested in combining scents for therapeutic purposes, the in-house aromatherapist will advise you. Bare Escentual Oils are sold in some specialty stores and are available by mail order. Call toll-free 1-800-227-3386 (outside California) and 800-227-3788 (in California).

If you would prefer to use a body lotion rather than an oil, there are dozens to choose from. Most of those sold in pharmacies and department stores are mineral oil based. These are fine provided that they are never used on the neck and face. People with very dry skin may find a mineral oil-based product preferable to a natural, vegetable, oil-based one, because they are more occlusive and are less expensive. This is not a product to be stingy with; it should be applied liberally, twice a day. My favorite product of this type is Nivea Skin Oil, which is sold in most pharmacies. It contains lanolin oil as well as mineral oil, which makes it very greasy. For this reason, it will completely camouflage even the most severe case of "alligator skin," although it won't cure it. If you like a shiny look on your bare legs in the summer, this is the product for you!

As for other mineral oil-based lotions, there is very little difference between them. You may choose the fragrance, price, or packaging you like best. Just remember that there is no therapeutic value to these products. *They work only while they are on your skin.*

In order for a lotion to *heal* dry skin, it must contain penetrating or water-binding ingredients such as lecithin, aloe vera, hyaluronic acid, shea (karite) butter, vitamins, or essential oils. Complex 15 Lotion, sold in pharmacies, is one of the best of these types of products because it is mineral oil free and contains a significant amount of lecithin. Its powerful water-binding ability is derived from the fact that it is a phospholipid, a substance able to bind 20 times its weight in water. Continued use of a product such as this actually helps to repair dry skin by increasing its ability to hold water. Some other brands, commonly recommended by dermatologists and sold over the counter in pharmacies, are Formula 405 Moisturizing Lotion, Lacticare Lotion, Neutrogena Emulsion, Neutrogena Body Lotion, Nutraderm Lotion, and Eucerin Unscented Moisturizing Creme or Lotion.

Lachydrin Lotion is a relatively new treatment product available by prescription only that is recommended for severe cases of dry skin and for problems such as psoriasis and eczema. It contains Alpha Hydroxy Acids, commonly referred to as "Fruit Acids," which are similar to Retinoic Acid (Retin A). Some dermatologists believe that fruit acids may be as beneficial as Retin A in the treatment of aging skin.

A health food store is the place to shop if you would prefer to use a natural vegetable oil based body lotion. Annemarie Borlind makes an excellent one called Body Balm, which contains aloe vera along with herbal and plant extracts. Some other recommended ones are Reviva Labs Seaweed Body Treatment Lotion, Botanee Hand and Body Lotion with Karite Nut Butter, Paul Penders Creamy Body Lotion, Nature's Gate Satin Soft Body Cream, Mountain Ocean's Skin Trip, Autumn-Harp Body Lotion, and Zia Cosmetics' Beautiful Body Lotion 1-800-334-SKIN.

8. **Don't** use "bath beads." These are made of chemical salt compounds mixed with mineral oil and fragrance and have no value to the skin. They may also cause dryness if they are not rinsed off thoroughly.

Daily Exfoliation

Whether you take a bath or a shower, it is important to remove the outer layer of dead, dry skin cells from your entire body, below the neck, each time. Dry skin builds up on the body, just as it does on the face, changing its texture and appearance. Dryness, flakiness, "snakeskin," or "alligator skin," and a general dull, sallow look may all result from improper exfoliation. Regardless of the method used, always be very gentle on the chest area as the skin here is sensitive and prone to broken capillaries.

There are several methods of exfoliation, though some are better than others: A **loofah** is the inside skeleton of a dried gourd that looks like a strange type of sponge. Like a sponge, it expands and softens when it comes in contact with water. Because it is rougher than a sponge, it makes an excellent exfoliant. The open structure of the fibers allows air to pass through, which makes a loofah less likely to gather bacteria than a sponge or wash cloth. A loofah should always be used wet, with circular, massaging motions. It is not necessary to use soap with a loofah. After each use, shake it out well and hang it up to dry. This helps to prevent mold and mildew from forming.

Loofahs are sold in pharmacies, health food stores, department stores, and bath shops in their original long shape, ranging in size from 10 to 36 inches. The longer ones make good back brushes. Loofahs are also available in smaller, hand-sized pieces or sewn together with terry cloth to make a loofah mitt. All types and sizes are equally effective. Choose the one best suited to your needs.

A **wash cloth** is my least favorite type of exfoliant. It is not abrasive enough to be effective and can be a source of bacteria if used more than once.

A **sponge** is my second least favorite type of exfoliant because it is usually not abrasive enough, can gather bacteria if not allowed to dry properly, and falls apart too fast.

Grainy or exfoliating soaps are bars of soap with some type of granules mixed into them. I do not recommend these because they are too drying.

Biweekly Exfoliation

AT-HOME BODY SLOUGHING

Biweekly exfoliation, or sloughing, is stronger than your daily cleansing. Because it helps to remove any residual buildup of dead skin and increases circulation, it plays an important part in an effective body regimen. Exfoliation is to your body skin what flossing is to your teeth.

Dry brushing is an excellent method of full-body exfoliation. In fact, it may be the most effective method available for at-home use because of the exceptional impact it has on circulation.

Dry brushing, as the name implies, is done with a dry brush on dry skin. It must be done before showering for approximately 5 minutes. You should begin brushing at the ankles, using short, sweeping motions toward the heart. Concentrate on areas of about 8 to 10 inches in length, moving up the body. Always brush in one direction only, toward the heart. Concentrate on the buttocks and upper thighs, especially if cellulite is present. You may want to ask a roommate or spouse to do your back for you.

When you first begin to use the dry brush, your skin may feel sensitive, but with subsequent use it will be less and less sensitive. Most people come to enjoy the feeling and find it quite invigorating, and the increase in circulation also gives your skin a healthy glow.

The brush used in dry brushing may be made of natural boar bristle, hemp, or synthetic fibers. Many of the dry brushes sold are too rough for the average skin. I tested several different types and brands and found the synthetic ones to be unbearably rough. Rope or hemp mitts are better than the synthetics but still quite rough. I recommend boar bristle brushes: They tend to be the softest and the most effective.

Many health food stores and bath shops sell dry brushes. However, one of my favorites is the old-fashioned style back brush. These are made of boar bristle with a detachable wooden handle. The brush head has a cloth handle so that it may be used in the hand, when detached from the handle. These are readily available in pharmacies, bath shops, and department stores and sell for about $6. You can also affix the brush head to the handle to brush or wash your back.

A **full-body scrub** is another method of exfoliation that calls for a grainy, scrub-type product. It is very easy to do while taking a shower. You may choose from the list of commercial products below, or make your own with the following recipe:

Mix together in a medium-sized, nonglass bowl:

½ cup plain yogurt
½ cup cornmeal
½ cup oatmeal
4 tablespoons honey

Stand in the shower and wet your body under the running water. Scoop a handful of the scrub mixture from the bowl and, using both hands, apply it to one of your ankles. It is best to use both hands to gently massage one leg at a time, moving from ankles up to thighs. Use a circular, massaging motion until your entire body has been covered. Work toward your heart, emphasizing the upward part of the motion. Remember to be extremely gentle on the chest area. Massage every inch of your body below the neck until all of the mixture is gone. This should take a total of 3 to 5 minutes. Step under the shower and rinse off completely with warm water. Follow with a cool rinse. Apply a body oil to your skin while it is damp, pat dry, then apply a body lotion. Your skin will be pink due to the increase of circulation, and should feel very smooth and soft.

Body Masks. To the best of my knowledge, the only cosmetics company to offer an at-home body mask is Borghese. Their Terme di Montecatini Fango has a base of the mineral-rich mud that is taken from Montecatini, Italy. However, giving yourself a complete body mask at home is messy and uncomfortable. After applying the cold mask to your body, you would either have to lie on a rubber sheet and huge bath towels, or in an empty bathtub for twenty minutes. If you have a private backyard you might enjoy a body mask on a warm day and rinse off without having to track mud through the house. Realistically, this type of mask may be alright for application on target areas such as breasts or thighs. As a general rule, I think that body masks are best applied in a salon.

BODY SLOUGHING PRODUCTS

Body Love's Amazing Grains	H
Clarins Exfoliating Body-Scrub	DS
Naturade Aloe Lotion Scrub	H
Reviva Labs Honey and Almond Scrub	H
Terme di Montecatini Stimulating Body Refiner	DS

SALON BODY SLOUGHING

Body brushing is almost exactly the same as the treatment you do at home. The only difference is that the back of your body receives full treatment. The practitioner may use more pressure than you would use on yourself and the full treatment takes about 20 minutes instead of 5. It's very much like getting a Swedish body massage except the masseuse uses a brush or rope mitt instead of her hands. Dry brushing is usually followed by the application of a soothing lotion.

Salt scrubs use either coarse, kosher salt or Dead Sea salt. The body is moistened, then massaged with the salt. Although it does a thorough job of removing dead skin and increasing circulation, this is not a treatment for everyone, as it is painful. Equally good results may be gained from any of the other methods mentioned here, without the discomfort of a salt scrub.

Seaweed wraps are the most gentle type of body sloughing. Their main purpose is to moisturize and detoxify the skin, but the active ingredients that dissolve dead skin cells make them excellent exfoliants.

A warm seaweed extract is either brushed or applied by hand to the entire body. The body is then covered with a light plastic sheet or similar waterproof covering and wrapped in warm blankets or towels for approximately 20 minutes. During this time, toxins are drawn from the skin, nutrients enter, and dead cells are dissolved.

Mud baths are one of the oldest types of body treatments known to man. The Egyptian, Aztec, and Mayan cultures all used them. The mud is usually made from volcanic ash taken from various sources around the world. It is mixed with water, very often from a mineral or hot spring, to form a thick mud. The mud is mixed in large tubs and is so thick that the body rests on the surface, rather than sinking.

To take a mud bath, you lie down on the mud, your head resting on a bath pillow. An assistant then covers your body with handfuls of mud, leaving only your face uncovered. A cold cloth is usually placed on your forehead and you are left for about 12 minutes. The heat of the mud is not uncomfortable and seems to penetrate very deeply into your body. For this reason the treatment has had great popularity with arthritis sufferers. Like seaweed, the active ingredients in the mud dissolve dead skin cells, making this an excellent body sloughing treatment.

BODY MASKS

Hot fango is a term derived from the Italian word *fango,* meaning "mud." This treatment uses a mixture of either mud or seaweed and paraffin. The mud or seaweed is mixed into melted paraffin, then poured onto large metal pans that look like huge cookie sheets. The mixture solidifies as it cools. Once this occurs, the slabs are reheated to about 102 degrees. For a hot fango treatment, you choose the area of the body that you wish to treat, for example, the neck and shoulders. You lie face down on a massage table and the assistant cuts a piece of the fango large enough to cover this area. The piece is then placed on your neck and shoulder area and gently pressed to help it conform to your body. The particular type of heat generated by this combination of ingredients is able to penetrate deeply to relieve tense, sore muscles.

Cold fangos are used to soothe skin that has a propensity for broken capillaries because it helps to constrict them. The cool mud can also temporarily take away redness caused by this condition. The treatment may also be used on swollen areas, such as the abdomen, ankles, or knees, to draw out the excess water and heat that cause swelling.

Special Treatments

Steam may be the most beneficial and relaxing treatment available in a health club. I also recommend the steam attachments available for home use. The moist heat is beneficial to the skin without being dehydrating. It helps to relax muscles, increase the flow of blood and oxygen to tissues, and rid the body of toxins. If eucalyptus oil is added to the steam source, it will have the additional benefit of opening sinus passages and purifying the air you breathe. Eucalyptus is a powerful antiseptic and can actually kill airborne germs. A 10-minute steam treatment may be taken daily.

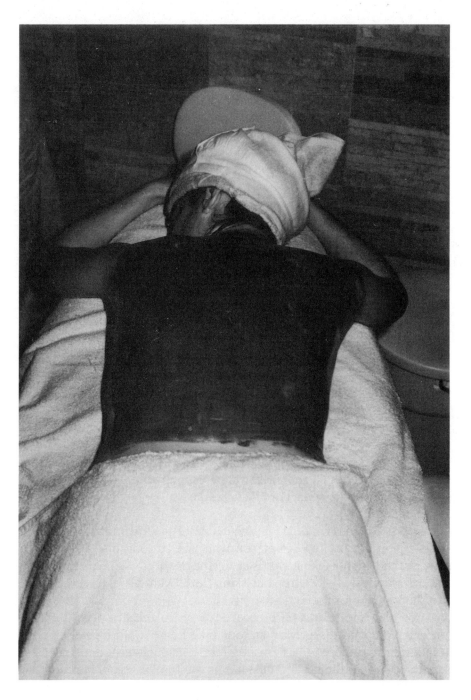

Cold fango, the Doral Saturnia International Spa Resort, Miami, Florida

There are several ways to enhance your steam experience and protect yourself from possible adverse effects:

- Always shower before steaming. This helps you to acclimate to the heat. It also helps your pores open faster.
- Always sit on a towel rather than directly on a bench in a steam room. Bacteria love wet heat.
- Steam naked if possible to allow more complete detoxification of pores.
- After 5 minutes in a steam room, use a loofah to gently massage dead cells from your skin. You may also use a pumice stone on rough elbows, feet, and callouses. Steam is an easy way to soften them.
- After steaming, wash your body well with a nondrying soap or gel to remove dead cells and toxins.
- Take a head-to-toe cool rinse after your shower to help close down pores and seal in warmth.
- Always apply a body oil and/or lotion following steaming and rinse to help seal in moisture.

Saunas may be damaging to skin because dry heat is dehydrating, but there are several things you can do to make a sauna less dehydrating:

- Pour water over the rocks to create a "wet sauna." Be aware that this also increases the temperature.
- Take a hot shower before taking a sauna to help your pores open more readily.
- Apply oil to your body before taking a sauna to protect your skin.
- Cover your face, neck, and chest with a damp towel.
- Never stay in a sauna for more than 12 minutes.

I do not recommend taking a sauna more than two or three times a week. If you are the type of person who takes a long time to begin to perspire, I advise not taking saunas at all. The dry heat will break capillaries and may seriously dehydrate your skin. Those with fair, thin skin should also shun saunas for the same reasons.

Hot tubs and Jacuzzis are excellent ways to relax, especially if you can enjoy them in the privacy of your own home. Unfortunately, public facilities, such as those in health clubs, may contain either too much or too little chlorine or bromine. Too little means you run the risk of infection and too much is dangerous to breathe because it irritates the lungs and can dry out the skin. Another characteristic of chlorine that you may have noticed is that the smell clings to your body, even after you shower. This is because chlorine bonds with urine and sweat to form chloramines, chemicals that adhere to the skin. However, there are two product lines that offer shampoos, soaps, and hair conditioners designed to remove chlorine from the skin and hair. Ultra Swim Anti-Chlorine Treatment Shampoo, Conditioner, and Soap are sold in pharmacies, and World Wide Aquatics, Inc. makes C-Free products based on vitamin C. Both of these product lines effectively neutralize chloramines. For information call 1-800-543-4459 or 1-800-582-2648 (in Ohio).

Deodorants and Antiperspirants

Perspiration is the way the body regulates temperature. The eccrine glands, located all over the body, excrete a clear, odorless substance that is free of organic matter. The apocrine glands, located in the armpits and genitals, produce organic matter, or toxic waste, which bacteria thrive on. It is these bacteria, which become trapped in moist body hair, that are responsible for body odor.

Deodorants may be the safest way to deal with body odor because they kill bacteria without interfering with the body's release of perspiration. When you realize that perspiration is supposed to leave the body, it doesn't make sense to prevent this. However, at the same time, heavy perspiration can be embarrassing and ruin clothing. People with this problem will most likely choose to use an antiperspirant. A person with light to moderate perspiration may need nothing more than a cornstarch based powder, such as Diaparene. Powders of this nature help to absorb moisture as it appears and are very effective.

An antiperspirant, on the other hand, works by inhibiting the flow of moisture from the body. The active ingredient enters the sweat ducts and forms a barrier. This barrier resembles a gelatinous glob and forms over a period of 7 to 10 days. The antiperspirant will not be effective until these barriers are in place and must then be used continually in order to maintain its effectiveness.

Most antiperspirants and deodorants contain aluminum compounds such as aluminum chlorohydrate and aluminum chloride. There is a great deal of evidence to show that aluminum contributes to various mental debilities, including Alzheimer's disease. Aluminum is also present in many toothpastes, as well as a host of prepared foods from pickles to nondairy coffee creamers, and is commonly added to public water supplies in the form of alum, where it helps to prevent cloudiness. I prefer to recommend natural, aluminum-free deodorants rather than antiperspirants. Three of my favorite brands are Yodora, by Norcliff Thayer, Inc., which may be found in a pharmacies, and Tom's and Pierre Cattier, which are available in a variety of fragrances and can be found in health food stores.

How to Be Odor-Free Without Chemicals

The most effective way to combat underarm odor is to keep the area as free of hair as possible. Shaving is not the most effective way to do this because it merely cuts the hair off at the skin line. The remaining stubble continues to grow and may be collecting bacteria in a matter of hours. It may also be irritating to apply a deodorant after shaving, so if you shave in the morning, you would be unprotected all day. If you shave at night, bacteria-grabbing stubble has returned by morning.

The most effective hair removal treatment is waxing. It removes the hair by the root so that it must grow out completely. This takes approximately 28 days. Because it has not been cut off in mid-shaft, the hair grows in soft rather than stubbly. Another advantage of waxing is that less hair grows back each time. After several years of waxing you will have very little hair. If you wax at night deodorant may be applied the next day, with no irritation. However, most women find that waxing eliminates the need to use a deodorant until the hair has begun to grow back.

There are two types of wax treatments that are appropriate for use at home. But before you attempt to wax yourself, I recommend having two or three professional treatments. This will familiarize you with correct waxing techniques and equipment. You may even decide to continue with professional waxing, instead of at-home treatments. Fees for a professional waxing usually range from $8 to $14. This is quite reasonable considering that you will need treatment only every 4 to 6 weeks.

Several brands of hot wax are sold at beauty supply stores for at-home use. The most popular one, and easiest to find, is called Honnee Wax. However, my favorite is L'Orbette, but it is not as readily available in some areas.

Sally Hansen's Cold Wax may be purchased at most pharmacies. It is convenient for travel and easy to use because it is applied directly from a tube and does not require heating. However, it pulls the hair more than hot wax, and for this reason I would not recommend it to novice waxers. A new brand of cold wax, Atta Lavi, is much more gentle and easier to use. It is sold in health food stores and available directly from the manufacturer, Atta Lavi, 1168B Massachusetts Avenue, Cambridge, MA 02138.

Your skin may feel a little tender after your first and second waxing treatments, but will become less sensitive with each treatment. You can reduce sensitivity and redness by applying a thin paste made of baking soda and water immediately after treatment. This will dry and leave a powdery film on the skin. Brush off the excess and let the remaining light film stay on your skin for several hours or overnight. This effective postwaxing treatment may be used on any part of your body.

There is another way to eliminate underarm odor without using harsh chemicals. A product called Lavilin, which is based on the herbs calendula and arnica, was recently introduced in this country. It is unique because of its effectiveness in killing odor-causing bacteria. Once bacteria have been eliminated, it takes as long as 15 days for them to regenerate and until this occurs, your body is odor-free. The product need only be applied when bacteria return—every 5 to 15 days. Lavilin is unconditionally guaranteed and sold in health food stores or by mail order. The toll-free number is 1-800-LAVILIN.

Sun Sense

For those of you not yet aware of the link between sunlight and aging, the following statement may be shocking: Exposure to ultraviolet rays from the sun is the major cause of skin aging. If you doubt the truth of this statement, please test it yourself by getting undressed and closely observing the skin on the underside of your breast or upper arm. Then compare it to the skin on the back of your hand. The only difference is the amount of sun exposure these areas receive. As you grow older, the hidden skin under the breast and arm, and on any other area not exposed to ultraviolet light, will remain unchanged. Unprotected areas such as the hands, face, and neck will develop lines and wrinkles, age spots, lose their elasticity, and change their texture. These skin changes occur as a result of *incidental* exposure to the sun: walking outside, driving, playing sports, gardening, etc. A person who sunbathes *intentionally* will develop the type of skin which facialists refer to as "elephant skin." Picture an older woman who has spent years of winters in Florida. In her youth she may have been described as being "brown as a berry." Past the age of 45 or 50, she may be compared to a walnut. *This type of skin aging is not inevitable.* It is a direct result of exposure to sunlight and can be avoided by proper protection.

If you think that you are still too young to be concerned with aging, maybe these facts will make you think twice about getting a tan: In 1935 only 1 out of every 1,500 Americans could expect to develop malignant melanoma, the most deadly type of skin cancer. In 1985 the odds changed to 1 in 150. The American Academy of Dermatology estimates that by the year 2000 the number will have risen to 1 in 100. Although genetic inheritance can create a predisposition to melanoma, this type of skin cancer most often affects those who experienced damaging sunburns as teenagers.

The American Cancer Society estimates that 500,000 Americans will also develop the more common types of skin cancer—squamous and basal cell carcinoma. These types of skin cancers afflict those people who are most often exposed to sunlight. The Society also advised me that this number is most probably lower than the actual figure due to inaccurate reporting of treatment by dermatologists.

One of the worst aspects of sun damage is the fact that it is cumulative. A person may tan for the first 25 years of his or her life without noticing any ill effects. Then "suddenly" the skin changes and begins to age. The best analogy I've ever heard regarding this was given on national television by a dermatologist who likened suntanning to the boiling of an egg. A raw egg may be submerged in boiling water for a few seconds with no apparent change. Submerge it for a few more seconds and there is still no change. But if you continue to submerge it, for just a few seconds at a time, after several minutes, it will become hard-boiled.

Many people use tanning booths, believing them to be a safe way to acquire a tan. I am sorry to say that this is not true. Tanning booths are touted as being safe because they employ ultraviolet A rays rather than ultraviolet B rays, which are the ones that cause skin cancer. "A" rays are generally believed to be noncarcinogenic. However, they age the skin by inhibiting the production of collagen and elastin fibers, and unlike "B" rays, they can go through glass. In fact, recent research shows that tanning booths temporarily inhibit your body's natural repair process in healing damage caused by ultraviolet B rays. This means that if you expose your skin to the sun directly following a tanning booth treatment, you will not have the benefit of your body's natural protective mechanism.

I am not suggesting that you avoid the sun completely, but rather that you protect yourself from its harmful rays. There are several things you can do to enjoy the sun safely:

1. Wear a sunblock with SPF (sun protection factor) #15 or more, on a daily basis during sunny weather. Apply the block 15 to 30 minutes before going in the sun to be sure it is working before your skin is exposed. Be aware of how long the block will protect you. To determine this, multiply the SPF number by the amount of time you can stay

in the sun unprotected before you begin to burn. For fair skin types this is usually 10 minutes. Darker skin types may be up to 20 minutes. Use the block on all exposed skin including face, neck, ears, arms, and hands. If you have combination or oily skin, choose an oil-free block from the list below:

Note: I do not recommend any sun care products that contain PABA (para-aminobenzoic acid) because it is a known sensitizer and a possible carcinogen. Tests conducted by Dr. Thomas Fitzpatrick, M.D., Ph.D., chairman of the Department of Dermatology at Harvard University Medical School, show that PABA caused mutagenic changes in the cells of mice.

OIL-FREE SUN BLOCKS

Aloe Up Super Block SPF 25 (waterproof)	P, M*
Bull Frog SPF 36 (waterproof)	P, H
Burn-Off SPF 16 (waterproof)	P, M**
Clinique Oil-Free Sun Block SPF 15	DS
Dorsey Laboratories Total Eclipse SPF 15	P
Germaine Monteil's Oil-free #15	DS
Lil Gator SPF 25 (waterproof)	P, H
Prescriptives Oil-Free SPF 15 Sun Protection	DS
Prescriptives Oil-Free SPF 19 Sun Protection	DS
Solbar PF Liquid 15 Clear Paba Free Sunscreen	P

*Aloe Up, P.O. Box 2913, Harlingen, TX 78551
**Burn-Off Corporation, P.O. Box 166767, Irving, TX 75016. Call toll-free, 1-800-531-5731

If you have normal or dry skin, you may prefer an oil-based sunblock because they are less drying. For the face and neck I recommend the following natural oil-based blocks rather than mineral oil-based ones:

OIL-BASED SUNBLOCKS

Aloe Up Suntan Lotion SPF 20	P, M*
Clinique Face-Zone Sun Block SPF 15	DS
Dr. Linda Sy Fang's Non-PABA Sunblock SPF 15	M
Coppertone Water Babies (Waterproof)	P
Estée Lauder Total Sunblock Cream SPF 23 (tinted)	DS
Estée Lauder Super Sun Block SPF 20	DS
Lilly of the Desert Skin Saver Sunblock SPF #40 (waterproof)	H
Mountain Ocean Sunblock SPF 15	H
Neutrogena PABA Free Sun Screen #15	P
Prescriptives Sunblock H SPF #23	DS

Prescriptives Sunblock #15	DS
Repechage Maximum Protection Sunscreen SPF 15	S
T-1 Screen SPF 15 Plus (PABA free)	P, D

*Aloe Up, P.O. Box 2913, Harlingen, TX 78551

Mineral oil based sunblocks are fine to use on all parts of the body except the face and neck. Fortunately, there are many good products to choose from that do not contain mineral oil.

2. Use a waterproof sunblock when swimming.
3. Wear a hat.
4. Wear sunglasses with UV protective lenses. The fact that these are now readily available in department stores and pharmacies illustrates the public's growing concern with sun protection.
5. Sit under a beach umbrella or in the shade to safely enjoy a day at the beach or a picnic.
6. Cover your arms and legs with light, cotton clothing when walking, jogging, or bicycling in the sun for periods longer than a sunblock will protect you.
7. Walk on the shady side of the street and sit in the shady section of outdoor restaurants. Remember that not only are sunbathing and swimming dangerous times in the sun—every minute of sun exposure counts. If you are walking, driving, gardening, or doing anything in the sun, your skin must be protected.

If you want the look of a tan without the damage, you may want to try a self-tanning cream. These new products, first introduced to the American market in 1985, bear no resemblance to their counterparts of the sixties: Man-Tan and QT. If you ever tried one of those you'll remember that they turned your skin orange. The newer products are white lotions that are applied in the same way as a body lotion. A few hours after application, the skin darkens as a result of the chemical reaction that has taken place in the outer layers. The tan color won't rub or wash off and fades in several days, much like a real tan.

Before using one of these products on your face, try it on your body, as the color may fade unevenly. Fading is not readily noticed on legs and arms. Also, self-tanning creams may contain mineral oil or other undesirable chemicals that can cause clogged pores or breakouts on the face, but won't affect the rest of the body's skin.

Three of my favorite brands of self-tanning creams sold in department stores are Estée Lauder Self-Action Tanning Creme, Elizabeth Arden's Sun Science Self-Tanning Lotion, and Clarins Self Tanning Milk. Zia Cosmetics also offers one called Sans Sun Self Tanning Creme that is available in health food stores and by mail order. For ordering information call 1-800-334-SKIN or write to Zia Cosmetics, P.O. Box 143, Mill Valley, CA 94941.

I do not recommend self-tanning products that contain walnut oil as a primary ingredient because they simply stain the skin. They also create an orange tan and can cause dark patches that linger for as long as several months. Unfortunately, all of the "natural" self-tanning creams that I tested contained walnut oil.

Don't be tempted by the "tanning pills" advertised in magazines and health food stores. They contain high amounts of beta-carotene, which also causes the skin to turn orange. Another popular ingredient in these pills is canthaxanthin, which is not approved as a food additive by the FDA. Both of these ingredients may also cause liver damage.

CHAPTER
FOUR

BODY TONING AND DETOXIFICATION

In order to keep your body in proper shape, that is, skin taut, muscles firm and supple, it is necessary to "tone" your muscles by some means of exercise. Passive exercise machines such as those being used in body treatment salons are becoming more popular and are effective for this purpose; however, they offer no aerobic or cardiovascular benefits, as exercise does. Aerobic exercise helps to improve circulation, increase oxygen intake, boost collagen production, and relieve stress symptoms. For these reasons, I recommend active exercise, rather than passive, although passive treatments may be used in conjunction with a regular, active exercise program to relieve trouble spots of cellulite (as discussed later in this chapter).

The removal of toxins from the body (detoxification) is as important as toning in helping to prevent excess water and trapped toxins from causing problems such as bloating, blemishes, cellulite, tiredness, irritability, and poor circulation. If your body is retaining water or toxins, you will never achieve optimal body tone by exercise alone, although exercise does help your body to release some toxins through perspiration. However, both water retention and toxic pollution may also be treated from the inside by the use of nutritional supplements and natural diuretics.

Water retention is primarily a result of a lack of potassium, which regulates the water balance in cells. A potassium deficiency is commonly caused by an excess of sodium, or salt. Suggestions for how to effectively cut down on the amount of salt in your diet were outlined in Chapter 2.

Although many doctors prescribe diuretic pills as a cure for water retention, these substances can add to the core of the problem by robbing the body of potassium. A sufficient daily intake of potassium will help your body maintain an even cell-water level balance. All fruits and vegetables contain potassium. Bananas, dark green leafy vegetables, dried apricots, potatoes (including the skin), dairy products, whole grains, dried beans, sunflower seeds, and garbanzo beans are excellent sources of potassium.

In addition, pyridoxine, vitamin B_6, also helps the body to maintain the proper sodium/potassium balance. It is recommended that 100 mg of B_6 be taken daily as part of a vitamin B complex supplement. (Always check with your doctor or nutritionist before starting any vitamin regimen.)

Several fruits and vegetables are also good diuretics. When choosing fruits, melons are a particularly good choice but should be eaten alone, not in combination with other foods. After eating melon, be sure to wait one hour before eating another food. Grapes and pineapple are also very effective. In the vegetable category, parsley, cucumber, watercress, garlic, artichoke, and asparagus work well. Parsley juice is especially good and may be mixed with other vegetable juices, such as carrot or tomato.

In the case of water retention that is caused by the menstrual cycle, I recommend drinking a variety of herbal teas. All herbal teas are natural diuretics, although some are stronger than others. Two of the best are Crystal Star's Lean and Clean, and Naturode's K-B 11. Both contain detoxifying herbs and are sold in health food stores. Other particularly strong diuretic teas are alfalfa leaf, raspberry leaf, and hibiscus. Three cups per day are sufficient for a diuretic effect, although you may drink as many cups of herbal tea as you like.

By incorporating diuretic fruits, vegetables and foods high in potassium into your diet, you help to maintain the proper water balance in your body. You may also choose to do a weekly or monthly inner cleansing by eating only combinations of these special foods for one day. A good combination might be melons for breakfast, grapes, pineapple, and banana for lunch, and a dinner of artichoke and asparagus, with a salad of cucumber, watercress, sunflower seeds, and parsley. Remember to drink lots of cold, sodium-free water and herbal teas, too. Contrary to what may seem logical, drinking a lot of water does not cause bloating unless you also eat a lot of salt. In fact, if you don't drink a sufficient amount of water, your body will retain the water it already has, acting as if there is a shortage. Drinking six to eight glasses of sodium-free water daily helps to flush toxins from your body and keep the water level in your cells balanced.

An inexpensive way to provide yourself with pure drinking water is to purchase a Brita water filter. The small filter is housed in its own glass or plastic pitcher and sells for about $30 in health food stores.

Toxins and toxic wastes that remain in the body are harmful in two different ways: (1) they start chemical reactions that ultimately produce free radicals, the substances responsible for the breakdown of cells, which leads to aging and sickness, and (2) the body's defense mechanisms surround toxins with fluids and fats in an attempt to render them harmless. These globules of "protected" toxins form the basis of the lumps and bumps we know as cellulite. As I mentioned in Chapter 2, free radicals are best neutralized by the ingestion of certain vitamins and minerals. When vitamins A, B_1, B_2, B_3, B_5, B_6, B_{12}, C, D, E, and zinc are taken in conjunction with whole fresh foods, these supplements supply the best way to tone your body from the inside.

Selenium is another important ingredient in this program. It is a trace mineral (only needed in small amounts) and a powerful antioxidant that helps cells to release toxins. Some foods high in selenium are seafood (especially tuna), onions, whole grains, bran, wheat germ, tomatoes, cabbage, and broccoli. Selenium is often incorporated in multivitamin supplements, but should not be taken by itself unless prescribed by a nutritionist or doctor.

Ridding the body of toxins once they have been surrounded by fat can be very difficult. You must start the process from the inside by adjusting your diet and adding supplements to fight oxidation and remove free radicals. But there are also many treatments for the outer body. These range from detoxifying baths to special types of massage. I will discuss each in detail to help you decide which one is right for you.

Aromatherapy and Lymphatic Massage

Aromatherapy evolved from the oldest form of medicine known to man. Aromatherapy is based on the usage of plant extracts, currently called botanicals or essential oils. The first evidence of the usage of plant-based substances dates back to the Neanderthal man, who used them medicinally. The Chinese employed the technique two thousand years before the birth of Christ and the Egyptians used plant-derived resins and oils in cosmetics, medicinals, incense, and embalming. But the Greek Theophrastus is acknowledged as the first "aromatherapist" for his experiments with aromatics (plant-derived extracts) and their effect on thinking, feeling, and health.

By the third century A.D., the Romans had developed and expanded the usage of aromatics, making them an integral part of pleasure as well as health. During this time, fragrant oils were commonly used in baths and perfumes, and for massage.

The Arabs, Aztecs, French, Italians, English, and American Indians all used aromatics for medicinal and cosmetic purposes prior to the twentieth century. In 1910 a French chemist, René-Maurice Gattefosse, began extensive research into the curative powers of essential oils. His experiments were expanded upon by Dr. Jean Valnet and the biochemist Marguerite Maury. Madame Maury specialized in the application of essential oils for natural skin care. One of her students, Micheline Arcier, has further developed the usage of plant extracts into aromatherapy as we know it today.

The extracts used in aromatherapy are called essential oils, although they are not, in fact, oils, but rather volatile essences placed into a base of vegetable oil. Their natural composition allows them to penetrate the skin more thoroughly than other oils or water due to their chemical composition and the molecular breakdown that occurs as a result of extraction.

Several commercial cosmetic companies now offer lotions and oils containing essential oils and plant extracts that are designed for home use. Among them are Clarins, Biotherm, and Elancyl. On testing these products, I found that none had an effect on either water retention or cellulite. I believe this is because essential oils are effective only when combined with specific massage techniques that are not possible to do on oneself.

An aromatherapist uses various combinations of essential oils, along with an appropriate massage technique, to help detoxify a person's body by reestablishing the proper function of the lymphatic system. This is done with a series of treatments over a period of time.

It is important to have a properly functioning lymphatic system because it aids in the elimination of toxins and waste products. The colorless fluid in which toxins and waste are carried is called lymph. Lymph flows through the smallest blood vessels (capillaries) to larger ones, and finally arrives at the lymph glands or nodes where it is purified. During this process, the glands also use lymph to produce antibodies, which the body uses to fight infection. Once cleansed, lymph reenters the bloodstream and again begins its journey picking up toxins. However, unlike blood, which is pumped through our bodies by the heart, lymph has no pump but is moved by the movement of our bodies. Inactivity or a diet high in toxins can produce an oversaturation of lymphatic tissue and block the lymph glands. The trapped toxins may then become surrounded with fat as the body attempts to protect itself. They can also drain your energy and make you sick. Keeping the lymph flowing is one of the reasons why regular physical activity is so important to the maintenance of health and beauty.

There is an alternative to undergoing a series of professional aromatherapy massages and that is for you and a friend to learn the technique yourselves. Since the massage can't be done on your own body, you and your partner can take turns massaging each other. Judith Jackson, one of America's foremost aromatherapists, has written *Scentual Touch: A Personal Guide to Aromatherapy* (Henry Holt, 1986), an excellent book that teaches this massage technique as well as how to choose and formulate essential oils.

Thalassotherapy

The word *thalassotherapy* (in Greek, *thalassa* means "sea") was coined by the French doctor Bonnardière of Arcachon in 1869 to describe therapeutic bathing treatments involving seawater and seaweed. The practice has existed since before the birth of Christ. At that time, the Romans, who were particularly fond of bathing, frequented the town of Baiae on the Bay of Naples to take the therapeutic baths. Thalassotherapy has since been expanded to include a variety of other treatments such as body wraps and massages using seaweed and sea mud. The Americanized version of the word is *marineotherapy,* and often Europeans refer to it as *balneotherapy.*

Thalassotherapy spas have been popular in Europe for over two centuries. The first were built in England and Germany in 1792. French, Romanian, and Hungarian spas appeared a few years later. Although they have flourished in Europe, thalassotherapy spas have just recently been introduced in the United States. As of this writing, only two exist: Gurney's Inn on Montauk, Long Island, New York, and the Doral Saturnia International Spa Resort in Miami Beach, Florida. Both of these spas will be discussed at length in Chapter 11.

The theory behind thalassotherapy is that seawater, which has a chemical composition almost identical to that of human plasma (the fluid part of blood and lymph), contains all of the elements necessary for cellular life. In fact, experiments have shown seawater to be the only environment other than blood in which human white blood cells continue to live.

Seaweed absorbs seawater and retains its nutrients in a compact form with a density as high as ten thousand times greater than that of seawater. Since heating and dehydration destroy seaweed's active elements, a special process, *cryobroyage* (microburst under cold temperatures), had to be developed. The only place where this particular type of processing is done is the Goemar Laboratories, on the Brittany coast in Saint-Malo, France, which boasts one of the richest seaweed fields in the world. The cryobroyage process yields a concentrated, liquid seaweed cream whose particles are between 6 and 10 microns in size. This minute molecular structure allows the vitamins, minerals, trace elements, and amino acids to penetrate deeply into the skin. The best thalassotherapy treatments employ products that contain at least 90 percent seaweed concentrate. Body products such as lotions and creams, designed to be used following treatments and at home, should contain a minimum of 15 percent seaweed concentrate in order to be effective.

The following list will give you an idea of the components of seaweed and its benefits for your skin:

- Amino acids aid in tissue development and reconstruction.
- Mineral salts help increase cell vitality, increase the skin's ability to hold moisture, and regulate overactive oil glands.
- Trace elements help to rid the skin of toxins and neutralize free radicals.
- Iodine (found in abundance in the thyroid gland) helps to regulate metabolism, activates blood circulation, and revitalizes cells.
- Magnesium has a moisturizing effect.
- Vitamins nourish the skin, compensate for deficiency, and help boost cell production.
- Concentrated seaweed is a natural exfoliant that rids the skin of dead cells.

At-Home Thalassotherapy Treatments

There are several products that you can use at home to turn your bathtub into a spa. Taking a seaweed bath is incredibly relaxing, as well as being good for your skin. It is an excellent antidote for aching muscles and helps your body release toxins. The companies that offer this type of product claim that if used once a day, over a period of several weeks, it will also have a slimming effect on the body. Although this may be possible—as a result of the release of toxins and increased circulation—results may not be obvious unless the bath treatments are combined with a program of diet and exercise.

The following products contain at least 90 percent seaweed concentrate and are sold in salons, spas, and cosmetic specialty stores: Florimar's Bain Non-Moussant (Nonfoaming Bath), and Repechage Reenergizing Seaweed Bath Spa-Style Treatment.

These product lines also offer full lines of body care products, including shower gel, soap, body lotion, and moisturizing creams, based on seaweed extract.

To achieve the best results I recommend dry brushing your body before bathing. This removes dead skin cells and revs up your circulation, so that nutrients in the bath water will penetrate more deeply. Follow the directions on the package regarding bath water temperature and the length of time that you should soak; times range between 15 and 30 minutes. If you want to relax following the bath, apply a seaweed-based lotion or cream to your body. Then wrap yourself in a warm robe or flannel sheet and lie down for 20 minutes. This is also one of the best anti-stress treatments I have ever tried. Or, if you'd rather reenergize, take a cool shower then reapply the seaweed cream to your body.

Spa Thalassotherapy Treatments

As I mentioned previously, only two American spas offer full thalassotherapy treatments. Several spas currently offer limited treatments such as seaweed wraps or sea mud masks.

The seaweed wrap utilizes Goemar Labs' seaweed creme. The creme is first warmed and then applied to your body. You are then wrapped in a thin, plastic sheet and covered with either a special heated blanket or hot, wet towels. You remain in the wrap for approximately 20 minutes. During this time, the seaweed dissolves dead skin cells and draws toxins and excess water from your skin. After you are unwrapped and have showered off, you will be amazed at how soft and smooth your skin feels—this is the most gentle type of body exfoliation.

The following spas offer the seaweed wrap:

Gurney's Inn, Montauk, Long Island, NY

The Doral Saturnia International Spa Resort, Miami Beach, FL

The Norwich Inn & Spa, Route 32, Norwich, CT 06360

Cal-a-Vie Health Resort, 2249 Somerset Road, Vista, CA 92084

The Ponte Vedra Club, Ponte Vedra, FL 32082

I expect thalassotherapy to become very popular during the next few years, and it is possible that by the time you read this, other spas will have begun to expand their treatments.

Hydro Massage

Hydro massage is often placed in the category of thalassotherapy, but this is only accurate if seawater is used in place of plain water. Currently, Gurney's Inn is the only spa in the United States that uses seawater for this treatment.

Hydro therapy massage is done in a large tub filled with water whose temperature is slightly higher than that of the body. The newer tubs are designed in either Italy or Germany and have dozens of Jacuzzi jets built into their sides and bottom. During the first phase of a hydro massage, you lie comfortably in the tub for 5 to 10 minutes while the jets gently help your muscles to relax. In the second phase, a masseuse uses water from an underwater hose to massage every inch of your body, beginning with your feet and moving up. The water pressure of the hose is adjusted to your comfort level and the overall effect is a painless deep-muscle massage. Treatment lasts from 30 to 60 minutes, varying from spa to spa. Although some people prefer the hand–body contact of traditional massage, to my mind, hydro massage is the most comfortable deep-muscle treatment. I feel that the masseuse is able to work much deeper with the water than would be comfortable with her hands.

Although hot tubs, Jacuzzis, and whirlpool baths can be relaxing, they are not considered to be hydrotherapy because there is no practitioner or masseuse manipulating your body in any particular way.

Herbal Wraps

Herbal wraps were initially introduced as instant slimming treatments and are not designed for use at home. Some salons and spas still advertise them as a way to lose inches in just one treatment. The problem is that all you really lose is water. As soon as you drink your first glass of liquid or eat a fruit or vegetable, the lost inches will reappear. Herbal wraps can be relaxing, provided you do not feel claustrophobic when you are wrapped up like a mummy!

Several different types of herbal mixtures are used in this treatment. The herbs help to pull toxins from the skin and may also act as mild exfoliants, depending on the combination that is used. During an herbal wrap, gauze strips are soaked in an herbal "tea," then applied to the body. Saran Wrap may be used over the gauze to hold in the moisture and make your body sweat. Cotton or wool blankets go over the wrap to hold in the heat. You rest in your cocoon for 20 to 30 minutes, then shower off. But an herbal wrap is not as effective as a seaweed wrap.

C H A P T E R
FIVE

LIPOSUCTION

Liposuction, the new method of removing lumps and bulges of unwanted fat, may be the answer to many women's prayers. Also referred to as "fat sucking," it removes localized fat deposits from the hips, thighs, buttocks, stomach, chin, neck, knees, arms, and ankles. It is used for deposits that are not affected by diet or exercise, but are a result of heredity, rather than overeating. Although most operations need only remove two to seven pounds of fat to achieve optimum results, patients lose inches and may drop as much as four clothing sizes.

Unknown in this country until 1983, liposuction was originally pioneered in the early 1970s in Italy by Dr. Georgio Fischer, an otolaryngologist (an ear, nose, and throat doctor). His idea was correct, but his method employed a sharp instrument that caused too much bleeding and fluid loss. A few years later, his idea was adapted by the French gynecologist Dr. Yves-Gerard Illouz, who perfected the treatment by using a blunt instrument. The new process was called blunt suction lipectomy. Dr. Illouz practiced for several years, performing over five thousand operations, before beginning to train other physicians in the method. Dr. Julius Newman, an American otolaryngologist practicing in Philadelphia, was one of the first to use the procedure in this country and coined the term *liposuction*.

Recently introduced to this country, liposuction has become the number one cosmetic/surgical procedure. In 1986 one hundred thousand patients were treated with liposuction. These figures make more sense if you consider the fact that over 80 percent of the female population of the United States consider themselves to be misshapen. Liposuction is also considered to be the safest of all surgical procedures—only four deaths have occurred as a direct result of the operation.

Because liposuction is much faster than the old method of carefully scraping fat cells away from the skin by hand, the technique is also used in conjunction with other types of cosmetic surgery such as face-lifts, chin tucks, tummy tucks, and breast reduction. This minimizes the amount of time a patient is on the operating table, which is better for both the patient and the physician.

The Dream Operation: What It Can and Can't Do

In its original form, liposuction was not designed to treat the problem of obesity. In fact, Dr. Alan Gaynor, a San Francisco dermatologist and one of the foremost American practitioners of liposuction, states that he will not perform the operation on anyone who is more than 20 pounds overweight. However, Dr. Michael Elam, of Newport Beach, California, believes that the procedure may have an effect on the way the body metabolizes fat—the removal of excessive fat enables the body to metabolize the remaining fat faster. He also believes he has proven that liposuction is "psychologically rewarding" and gives obese patients a "head start" on weight loss. In 1980, Dr. Elam performed liposuction on 200 obese patients, and follow-up studies show that all either maintained or lost weight during the year

Hips, thighs and buttocks before liposuction (Dr. Alan Gaynor)

Hips, thighs, and buttocks after liposuction (Dr. Alan Gaynor)

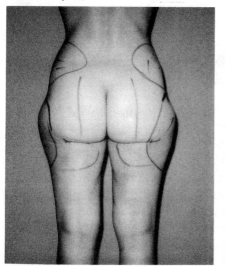
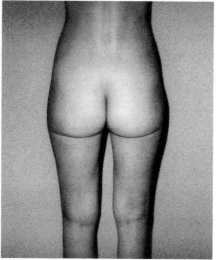

following the operation. Whether it is used as a cure for obesity or to create a more perfect figure, one of its biggest advantages is that the change is permanent. Once fat cells have been removed, they cannot replace themselves. Theoretically, fat can no longer accumulate in that area. It's important to note, however, that the remaining fat cells, although at a "normal" level, can expand if the patient gains a substantial amount of weight. In other words, liposuction does not allow patients to overeat without consequences.

The Controversy: Who Is Qualified to Perform Liposuction?

Liposuction may be performed by any physician with prior surgical training: a plastic surgeon, orthopedic surgeon, dermatologist, otolaryngologist, general surgeon, or gynecologist. The fact that no other requirements qualify a physician to practice liposuction has led to controversy within the medical community. Because the only requirement is that the doctor have prior surgical training, it is difficult for the general public to find a qualified liposuction surgeon.

Presently, any qualified doctor may take a 3-day course in liposuction from the American Society of Liposuction Surgery in Philadelphia or another similar teaching organization. This type of course trains in preoperative, operative, and postoperative procedures, and includes guidelines for choosing prospective patients. The American Society of Liposuction Surgeons also offers an observational fellowship program, which includes four one-week sessions with four different doctors who are proficient in liposuction surgery. The student doctor spends one week observing every phase of the operation, including the choosing of patients. In this way, he or she gets to experience many different types of liposuction operations, patients, and procedure methods.

Doctors are also taught how to analyze whether lumps and bumps under the skin are fat or muscle. If they are muscle, the problem is inoperable and the person is not a candidate. If the analysis is improperly made, and a person is taken as a candidate, there will be no excess fat available for suctioning and the operation will be a failure. The surgical procedure may not harm the patient, but the lumps and bumps will persist.

Unfortunately, no liposuction course in America includes hands-on operating techniques. At first this seemed ludicrous to me. I did not understand how anyone could learn to perform surgery simply by watching someone else do it. Dr. Julius Newman explained that this is normally the case with any new type of surgery (including laser surgery), largely because doctors are not licensed to practice in any state other than their own. If a doctor attends a seminar in another state, he may only observe operating procedure. There is also the problem of finding patients willing to undergo an operation at the hands of a student. Since hospital and insurance costs have climbed so high in recent years, surgical clinics have diminished. They still exist for medical and surgical students, but the emphasis is on reconstructive, rather than cosmetic, operations. I asked if cadavers were an option, as they are commonly used as practice for medical students, and was told that it wasn't possible to use them for liposuction. However, Dr. Newman assured me that liposuction was a simple procedure in itself, and that operating procedures such as monitoring fluid loss and replacement were the real keys to a successful operation. On the other hand, Dr. Gaynor disagreed vehemently with this and told me that learning the procedure seems "deceptively easy," adding that after performing more than 1,000 liposuction surgeries he still "feels like a novice."

Abdomen, before liposuction (Dr. Alan Gaynor)

Abdomen, after liposuction (Dr. Alan Gaynor)

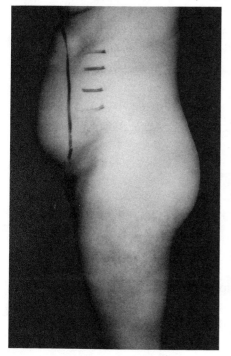
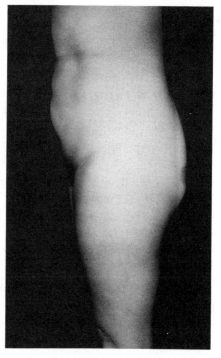

Because Europe does not have the same laws governing the practice of doctors, American physicians often go there to get experience. Dr. Gaynor is one American doctor who has spent time in practice with Dr. Illouz in Paris. He feels that this training was invaluable and has helped him to avoid many mistakes.

Another aspect of the controversy is which type of doctor is most qualified to perform liposuction. The American Board of Plastic and Reconstructive Surgeons thinks that plastic surgeons should be the only ones allowed to perform this operation. Drs. Newman and Gaynor point out that as specialists in their fields, they received an equivalent or greater amount of surgical training as residents than plastic surgeons. It is important to consider the fact that specialists routinely perform operations in their field of expertise, which gives them much more experience in those areas of the body related to their specialty than a plastic surgeon. For example, a gynecologist, such as the original founder of suction lipectomy, sees women's abdomens, buttocks, and hips on a daily basis. If anyone is exposed to every type of shape and size, it is he. Thus a gynecologist may be more qualified to make an aesthetic decision about how to properly shape a woman's body than a plastic surgeon who works mainly on faces or breasts. And an orthopedic surgeon certainly has more experience working with people's feet, knees, and legs than does a plastic surgeon.

It is important to remember that regardless of what type of doctor performs your liposuction, he or she should be well-trained in the procedure and have had extensive hands-on experience.

Are You a Candidate?

The general guidelines for a good liposuction patient state the following: The patient should:

- not be more than 20 pounds overweight
- have good skin elasticity
- have good muscle tone
- be psychologically stable
- be realistic about what the operation can do

Not everyone is a candidate for liposuction. Those with poor skin and poor muscle tone are the least likely candidates, unless they are willing to trade sagging skin for their lumps of fat. In one private consultation, an experienced doctor will be able to tell you immediately whether or not you fulfill their requirements as a candidate for liposuction. A consultation such as this may be free or cost as much as $150.

How the Operation Is Performed

The procedure may be done in a doctor's office–operating facility or in a hospital, and depending on the area to be treated, may be performed under local or general anesthesia. If a large area is to be suctioned, the physician may require the patient to spend the night in a hospital.

A tiny incision, ¼ to ½ inch long, is made in an area where it won't be noticed later, such as in the crease under the buttocks, the pubic hair, the navel, or under the arm. A long, thin, hollow stainless steel instrument, called a cannula, is inserted into the incision and moved back and forth to loosen the fat. The cannula makes channels in the fatty tissue that lies between the skin and muscles and carries the loosened fat out via a vacuum suction device attached to it. The surgeon creates a honeycomb of channels, rather than removing the fat totally, which could cause the skin to collapse. The operation may last between 30 minutes and 2 hours, depending on the size of the area being treated. Immediately following the suctioning, the patient is wrapped in elastic surgical tape and/or placed in a tight-fitting elastic girdle. This is left in place for approximately 7 to 10 days to help shape the new figure. Following buttock, hip, stomach, and thigh operations, a long-leg girdle must be worn for as long as several weeks. As the body heals, and with the help of the bandages and/or girdle, the empty channels that have been made under the skin compress, creating a smaller overall form.

The Recovery

The patients I interviewed experienced various lengths of recovery and degrees of discomfort. One patient was operated on on a Friday and went back to work the following Tuesday. Several patients felt varying degrees of numbness for up to 3 months. Bruising varied from almost none to severe. Many patients said that the first few days were extremely uncomfortable because of bruising under the skin, even though they took prescribed painkillers such as Tylox or Tylenol with codeine. No drugs containing aspirin may be taken due to its anticoagulant properties. Many doctors also prescribe Valium to help patients sleep.

One man who had liposuction to remove "love handles" said the recovery was the most painful experience of his life. But none of the patients said they were sorry for having had the procedure; in fact, most said that they were so happy with the results that the pain was worth it.

How to Find the Right Doctor

Finding a qualified liposuction surgeon may be difficult. Until recently, I believed the most capable practitioners were those who received training under Dr. Illouz, in France. However, this is changing since American physicians who have become expert themselves have begun to train others.

The best way to identify a qualified practitioner is to ask the right questions. The best place to start is with someone you know who has undergone the procedure. But don't just take that person's word without drawing some conclusions of your own. Your personal impression and rapport with a physician is one of the most important factors to consider. When interviewing physicians, remember that you are considering them as much as they are considering you. I recommend that you interview a minimum of two doctors, preferably three, before making a decision.

The following questions will help you to learn more about the doctor you are considering:

- Where did you receive your liposuction training?
- How many liposuctions have you done, and on what parts of the body?
- May I interview two of your patients who have had the same procedure I'm considering?
- May I see before and after photos of liposuction surgeries that *you have performed?*

I tend to feel that I would not put myself in the hands of someone who had performed less than several hundred operations. It is the lack of training and experience that can lead to patient dissatisfaction and disfigurement. The most common complaints are disproportionate removal of fat and ridges. Ridges, caused by uneven removal of fat, occur in about 1 out of 300 cases and can happen even under the best of circumstances. Dr. Gaynor believes that the "wet method," injecting a saline solution into the area before suctioning, greatly reduces this possibility. He explains that saline helps to liquify fat, thus making it easier to remove. However, the proponents of the "dry method" argue that saline does not, in fact, liquify fat and that the added fluid makes accurate assessment of the area difficult. Unfortunately, there is no definitive answer as to which method is best. Doctors who get consistently good results are obviously using the method that works best for them.

If you don't know anyone in your area who has had liposuction surgery, you may want to write to the American Society of Lipo-suction Surgery, 1455 City Line Avenue, Philadelphia, PA 19151, or call 215-896-6677, for a referral list of doctors in your area who have received certification from that society. But remember, certification from a 3-day training program is not a substitute for experience. It is only a starting point. Liposuction training alone does not ensure that a doctor will be able to perform surgery successfully. By the same token, choosing a board-certified plastic surgeon who does not have extensive liposuction experience simply because of his credentials is also wrong.

As with any new surgical procedure, time alone will determine the worth of liposuction. To date, no long-term negative results have been observed. Liposuction appears to be a miracle operation for those people who have suffered through life being unhappy about or hampered by the way they look and unable to do anything about it. Although it is considered a "vanity" operation, interviews with patients show that a person who feels better about his or her appearance also performs more effectively in life.

CHAPTER
SIX

CELLULITE

Cellulite (pronounced sell-u-leet) may appear on the thighs, buttocks, stomach, knees, or upper arms. It gives the skin a bumpy, pocked appearance and is often called "orange peel skin," or "cottage cheese thighs." It is a condition that affects only females. The word *cellulite* is French, which literally translated means "inflammation of the cell." Despite years of research by scientists, cosmetic companies, facialists, doctors, and scores of others, there is absolutely no agreement as to what this malady truly is or how it can be treated.

The following statements have been published during the last 7 years in medical journals, fashion magazines, health magazines, and books. Some are true and some are false. They illustrate the extent of the controversy over cellulite.

- Cellulite is a unique physical problem with characteristics and treatments all its own.
- Cellulite is only a fancy name women have given to ordinary fat.
- Cellulite has nothing to do with being overweight.
- Being overweight is one of the initial reasons why cellulite forms.
- Cellulite is not affected by diet.
- A simple 14-day, low-fat, high-fiber diet will cure cellulite completely.
- Cellulite goes away when you lose weight but it is the last fat to disappear.
- To get rid of cellulite you have to reduce to 3 to 4 pounds less than your desired weight.
- Cellulite is not affected by exercise.

- Certain exercises, such as leg lifts, "tushy" squeezes, hip rolls, aerobics, race walking, and swimming, are sure cures.
- Isolated or spot exercises are not going to tackle cellulite directly.
- Cellulite is inherited. If your mother has it, you'll have it.
- Cellulite is not affected by massage.
- An anticellulite massage is the fastest cure. (Between 2 and 30 treatments are recommended, depending on the one you choose.)
- Cellulite will develop by the time a woman is 20 years old, rarely later.
- Cellulite develops as a woman ages—a result of the natural slowdown in circulation.
- Cellulite is a result of poor circulation.
- Cellulite is a result of poor nutrition.
- Cellulite is a result of water retention.
- Cellulite is a result of hormonal imbalance.
- Cellulite is an overconcentration of fat cells due to a chemical imbalance in the skin cells ... a localized disorder of the tissues.
- Cellulite is a different kind of fat.
- Cellulite is not fat.
- Cellulite is the same as any other body fat.
- Cellulite is trapped toxins.
- There is no such thing as cellulite.
- There is no cure for cellulite.

I have been researching cellulite for 7 years and it seems as if every 6 months some new "authority" is interviewed regarding new findings, or a new treatment. The authority usually proclaims that he or she has finally debunked the myths and found the solution to cellulite. These findings are diligently published in fashion and beauty magazines under such titles as "How to Banish Cellulite in Just 10 Days." I have spent the past year testing each of these theories along with its treatment. Most did not work; some did. The good news is that cellulite can be eliminated. The bad news is that there is no miracle cure.

The Truth About Cellulite

The most complete studies of the condition known as cellulite were made in the late 1970s in Germany by two teams of researchers. The first team, made up of Drs. Nurnberger and Muller, sought to find an explanation of why cellulite occurs only in females. In their study of the outer and inner structure of the skin, they discovered "standing fat-cell chambers" separated by vertical walls of connective tissue located in the uppermost layer of inner skin tissue. In analyzing the findings of Drs. Nurnberger and Muller, Dr. Samuel Hartley, Ph.D., a doctor of nutrition, describes the upper portion of these fat cells as "arc-shaped domes which are weak and more prone to fold and buckle under the pressures of excess weight, water retention or a sedentary lifestyle." He explains that "this, in turn, causes smaller compartments of fat cells (papillae adiposae) to then break up and cluster tightly just under the skin. This combination of standing fat-cell chambers and clusters of papillae adiposae are the very elements that create the change of appearance in the skin's surface that we know as cellulite." This is the most responsible explanation of cellulite that I have ever found, and the only one based on sound scientific evidence.

In further studies, Drs. Sherwitz and Braun-Falco discovered that the rippling effect of cellulite is caused by fluid retention in adipose (fatty) tissue. Not only do the fluids cause swelling, they carry toxic waste. When toxins become trapped, they cause the breakdown of collagen and elastin fibers. This combination of swollen fat cells filled with trapped fluids and toxins creates a blockage of circulation, which is the final cause of the cellulite problem. When cells are denied nutrients and oxygen due to poor or blocked circulation, they are unable to reproduce and function properly. This, in turn, causes a thinness in the connective tissue between cells and the upper layers of skin causing further development of cellulite. Dr. Hartley states that "while the actual direct cause of cellulite is the breakdown of the connective fibers, probably the biggest reason for this breakdown is poor blood circulation. Although toxic accumulation and fluid retention certainly are a major contributing factor to cellulite, it is poor blood circulation that ultimately creates the right environment for cellulite to develop and grow. Loss of blood flow to an area—whether caused by lack of exercise, too much sitting, clogged arteries, or nutrient deficiency— can have a disastrous impact on cellulite formation." And once a small amount of cellulite forms, it contributes to an even greater slowing down of circulation.

So, the causes of cellulite can be summarized as follows:

- genetic female fat-cell structure
- swelling of fat cells due to excess fat and fluids
- the breakdown of collagen and elastin connective fibers caused by trapped toxic waste, which results from poor circulation
- the thinning of cell walls and connective tissue due to a lack of nutrients (repair materials such as vitamins A, C, and E) and oxygen, which results from poor circulation

Causes and Cures

I first noticed the beginning of a cellulite condition on myself when I was 36 years old. At that time, I had not been exercising regularly for a couple of years and had gained 6 pounds. That may not seem like a lot of weight to many of you, but considering that I am five foot one and usually weigh 98 to 99 pounds, that's a whole dress size for me. I tried the Elancyl Active Toning Massage Method (the first over-the-counter treatment sold in department stores) and got no results. Although this treatment addressed the problem of poor circulation, it did not take the other causes of cellulite into consideration. Had I combined this with a diet and exercise program, I might have gotten results.

I then signed up for a series of 20 treatments with a cellulite masseuse. At the beginning of each treatment four small rubber pads containing electrodes were placed strategically on my buttocks and upper thighs. These emitted a current that made the muscles contract for several seconds, and then relax. (This works on the same principle as a passive exercise machine that tones your muscles while you do nothing.) Hot pads were then placed over the entire area. The masseuse explained that the heat helped to soften the fat. (I thought of what happens to chicken fat when it is cooked, and that seemed to make sense.) These were left in place for 20 minutes. The pads were removed and a cream applied to the area while the masseuse began the real work of "breaking up the hardened nodules of fat, water, and toxins." This was the most painful treatment I have ever had. Although it is called "cellulite massage," it contains none of the relaxing elements associated with massage of any other kind. In fact, I was black-and-blue and sore for the first 3 weeks of treatment. The pain alone should have made this the definitive cellulite treatment. However, the masseuse assured me that massage alone would not cure my problem; proper nutrition and exercise were equally important. She told me that in order to banish the cellulite completely, I needed to weigh 2 pounds less than my ideal weight and to do an aerobic type of exercise for 1 hour every other day.

Losing 8 pounds when you only weigh 105 can be very difficult. I don't believe in starvation diets, because I like food too much and the lost weight returns as soon as the diet ends. So I opted for the slower-but-surer method of diet modification. The biggest change was cutting down on the amount of fat I ate. At the time, I was very fond of cheeseburgers for lunch, steak and fries for dinner, butter on everything, chunks of cheese for daily snacks, eggs and/or cheese for breakfast, and cream sauces galore. I also drank two or three café lattés made with extra rich milk every day. When I looked at my diet carefully, I was appalled at the amount of fat it contained. Cutting out fat was an easy and effective way to cut calories and force my body to burn its stored fat. I was surprised at how quickly I lost my taste for butter, whipped cream, and cheese, which began to taste greasy to me.

I began an aerobics class and quickly became addicted, because I felt so good afterward. The first few weeks were killers, but when I began to see results, I wanted more. The combination of exercise, a low-fat diet, and the cellulite massage treatments did the trick. In about 10 weeks, I had lost my excess weight and the cellulite was gone. I continued eating right and exercising regularly for the next five years and the cellulite stayed away.

I did not develop cellulite again until I was 41 and several aspects of my life-style changed drastically. First, I moved from San Francisco to Chicago. This automatically made me less active during the winter. I didn't walk as much and there were no hills to climb. Second, I stopped my usual aerobic exercise program. Third, I agreed to write two books, one after another, in a 9-month period, which caused me to spend up to 10 hours a day *sitting* at my word processor. (I had never sat that much for that long.) I gained 4 pounds. Fourth, I was under the most stress I have ever experienced for any length of time. If we examine these life-style changes more closely, they look like this:

- lack of exercise
- sedentary (job-related) habits
- overweight
- stress

Now look at how these relate to the causes of cellulite as listed earlier:

Lack of exercise = Poor circulation

Sedentary habits = Poor circulation

Overweight = Fluid and fat retention

Stress = Toxic waste and hormonal buildup

Two of these conditions, lack of exercise and overweight, were part of my earlier cellulite problem. Constant sitting and stress added further to the problem, making my new cellulite problem worse than my old one. I knew I could get rid of it in the same manner as before, but decided to make myself a guinea pig and try other methods first.

AT-HOME TREATMENTS:
WHAT WORKS, WHAT DOESN'T

Topical Treatments Topical treatments that promise results within 10 to 20 days are easy to use and may be used at home. I tried the Clarins line of products first, which includes two different body treatment oils: a contouring body cream, and a firming body cream. Each oil is designed to be used on a different part of the body, for either toning or firming. This was very confusing because every product label contained two or more of the following words: *toning, strengthening, firming,* and *contouring.* And although certain products were designed to be used together, there was no continuity in the labeling to let you know which to use with what or on what areas of the body. I had to decide which treatment was appropriate for the different areas of my body by following the guidelines on the backs of the bottles of oil. In the evening I used the Clarins Huile "Anti-Eau" Body Treatment Oil Contouring, Strengthening on my hips, thighs, and buttocks, followed by the Contouring Body Cream. In the morning, I applied the Clarins Huile Tonic Super Tonifant Body Treatment Oil Firming, Toning then the Firming Body Cream. Although these products feel wonderful on the skin, are well made, and contain natural oils and botanical extracts, I saw no change in the appearance of my cellulite. I had two other women test the same products and they also reported no change in the appearance of their cellulite.

I then tried the Biotherm 10-day treatment, which consisted of massaging the area twice a day, after showering, with a plastic hand massager, then applying a cream. In the instructions for the hand massager I was told to gently "walk" it up my buttocks a few times. It was obvious that this action did nothing to increase circulation because the skin did not turn pink, as it would have had circulation been increased. The cream was very similar to the one offered by Clarins. Results were promised in just 10 days, but once again, I saw no change. I continued using the product for another 2 weeks, but still saw no change. The saleswoman had offered a money-back guarantee, assuring me that no one had ever returned the product unsatisfied. Needless to say, I returned the unused portion for a full refund!

The Elancyl Active Toning Massage Method, mentioned earlier, is designed to be used in the shower. It consists of a nubbly, plastic massager containing a bar of "ivy extract" soap and is very effective for increasing circulation. Following bathing and massaging, an ivy extract cream is applied to the cellulite areas. At night, a green ivy extract gel is applied to the areas. The ivy supposedly penetrates the skin and acts to break up fat nodules and detoxify the area. Although the shower massage felt great, as did the cream and gel, none of us testing the procedure saw any difference in the appearance of our cellulite.

The next product I tried was Forever Living's Aloe Contour Cream. The distributors of this product told me to apply it to the cellulite area and then wrap the area with Glad Wrap. They said that this would be comfortable enough to wear all day, under my clothing. I was told that when I unwrapped myself after 6 to 8 hours I would see brownish globs of fat and toxins that had been drawn out by the cream. I applied the cream, which smelled like Noxzema, as instructed and wrapped myself in Glad Wrap. My skin began to heat up immediately. Although this did not hurt, it wasn't exactly comfortable. I wore a loose cotton dress over the wrapping that made a *swish-swish* sound when I walked. This sound, combined with the cream's strong menthol odor, certainly prevented me from leaving the house that day. After 5 hours I removed the wrapping and did not observe anything on my skin other than the melted, whitish cream that I had applied. My skin was very red, indicating an increase in circulation, and tingled when I showered off. It remained red for approximately 2 more hours, indicating that the cream had done an excellent job of increasing circulation. However, this seemed like a lot of trouble and discomfort to go through simply to increase circulation when dry brushing for 10 minutes would have been as effective.

I asked Baroness Hildegarde Von Mengersen, the director of Gurney's Inn on Montauk, Long Island, for her opinion of cellulite treatments. She told me that Gurney's had previously offered a 2-week cellulite treatment program but that very few people had been able to spend that much time at a spa. She felt that results would not be apparent with a shorter treatment, and that regardless of which method a person chose, success would depend on how religiously she continued to use it.

The Baroness explained the cause of cellulite as "slow metabolism in a specific area." She also stated that cellulite areas are usually cooler to the touch than the rest of the body, indicating an inadequate supply of blood and oxygen. Her recommendation for at-home treatment is a five-minute, once-a-day dry brushing of cellulite areas using a stiff-bristle brush with a brisk, sweeping motion toward the heart. This helps to increase circulation and correct the insufficient supplies of blood and oxygen. However, I don't believe that this has an effect on metabolism. She assured me that consistent practice of this technique would show results in 3 months. Her recommendation does agree with Dr. Hartley's assessments and would certainly help to improve circulation.

It seems a shame that most at-home treatments are sold as miracle cures rather than supplements to a full anticellulite treatment. Getting into the habit of massaging cellulite areas on a daily basis is an effective way to help prevent further formation of cellulite. But don't get discouraged—the results may not be evident for many months.

Seaweed Bath Treatments The seaweed bath treatment was the next one I tried. I had actually used this two years earlier for relaxation and detoxification and found it to be very pleasant. This treatment is based on another theory that cellulite is caused by trapped toxins. Toxins from such sources as drugs, artificial flavorings and preservatives, pesticides, hormones from red meat, or stress, alcohol, cigarettes, caffeine, and smog become lodged in fat cells as a result of improperly functioning lymph glands, inactivity, and lack of exercise. The toxins become entangled in collagen and elastin fibers, surrounded by fat, and form hard nodules or pockets. These cause the visible lumps and bumps that may also be felt. (This explanation, in part, closely resembles that of Drs. Sherwitz and Braun-Falco.) The seaweed extract penetrates the skin and helps to flush out toxins by the "depolarization" of fat cells. If this is, in fact, true, once the nodules are broken up, the visible characteristics of cellulite will disappear.

A seaweed bath is a very simple treatment and, as I mentioned earlier, it is also relaxing. Using the seaweed concentrate made by Goemar Laboratories, I added the powdered seaweed and calcium concentrates to a moderately hot tub of bath water and soaked for 20 minutes. If you are expecting a sweet-smelling tub of water when you try this, you will be greatly disappointed—there is no doubt that this is really seaweed because it smells like the bottom of the ocean. During the bath, use a rough loofah mitt to brush the cellulite areas to increase circulation. The bath should be taken twice a week for a minimum of 3 weeks, then once a week for maintenance. Results should be evident in 21 days.

Three other brands of seaweed baths were tested: Avancé, Repechage, and Florimar. Although all were relaxing and left the skin silky soft, no difference in cellulite was noticed by any of the women testing the products.

Inner Cleansing Inner cleansing, or detoxification, is often recommended as a supplement to the seaweed bath treatments. Many practitioners recommend two types of inner treatment: a calcium/magnesium supplement to combat stress and promote hormonal balance, and a natural diuretic to prevent water retention. Although you may already be aware of the importance of calcium—especially for its role in preventing osteoporosis—you may not be aware of the fact that most calcium supplements are difficult or impossible to digest. You may be taking the proper amount only to have it pass through your body undigested. Several supplemental calcium sources, such as bone meal and dolomite, may also contain high levels of lead. Although dairy products are an excellent source of calcium, they are also an excellent source of fat and cholesterol. For this reason, I recommend calcium/magnesium supplements that are derived from herbal sources or seaweed. The best herbal source of calcium is offered by Crystal Star Herbs, who also make herbal capsules and tea for cellulite treatment. These are available in health food stores. There are two brands of seaweed derived from calcium available—one made by Goemar Labs and sold under private label to health food stores, salons, and spas (Gurney's Inn offers this under their own Marino Vital label), and another sold by Spa Health under the Avancé label. To find out where the latter is sold in your area call 1-800-777-SKIN.

One of the simplest ways to alleviate water retention is to drink herbal teas. These are natural diuretics, and 2 to 3 cups a day will help your body maintain its proper water balance.

Dr. Hartley feels that it is especially important to have a diuretic in your system while you sleep to counteract fluid retention and decreased circulation. In his opinion, the most effective diuretics are those high in potassium, such as bananas and mushrooms. He also recommends taking vitamin B_6 (100 to 200 mg daily) because it helps to regulate the water level in cells by maintaining the proper potassium/sodium levels in your body.

Ionic Baths Machines that use electric stimulation are currently being tested for use in the treatment of cellulite. These are based on new research that indicates that the human body contains electromagnetic pathways similar to the veins and arteries that carry blood. This field of science is called bioelectricity and/or biomagnetism. The Swedish radiologist Dr. Bjorn Nordenstrom is one of the pioneers in this field. The book he published in 1983, *Biologically Closed Electric Circuits: Clinical, Experimental, and Theoretical Evidence for an Additional Circulatory System,* covered 2 decades of experimental work. According to Nordenstrom, we have an internal "electrical system" that works to balance the activity of our internal organs and initiates the healing process when an injury occurs. Current experiments are aimed at using electromagnetism for various types of healing.

One of the foremost American authorities on this subject is orthopedic surgeon Dr. Robert O. Becker, M.D., author of the book *The Body Electric: Electromagnetism and the Foundation of Life* (William Morrow, 1987). Dr.

Becker believes that bioelectricity has the ability to "heal injuries that we can't repair now, such as a severed spinal cord or damage to the heart muscle, injuries that almost never heal effectively." Ultimately, Dr. Becker speculates, this type of treatment may be used to help humans regenerate severed limbs. Presently, electrical stimulation is being used by hundreds of orthopedic surgeons to treat nonunion fractures, broken bones that will not heal.

Another area in which electromedicine has proven successful is the treatment of osteoporosis and osteonecrosis of bones. Dr. Arthur Pilla, Ph.D. is one of the pioneers in the field of electro-therapy who is currently doing research at New York's Mt. Zion Hospital. In 1975, Dr. Pilla developed a machine to promote the healing of bones. This same machine is now used by Helen Pappas at the Ageless Beauty Salon in New York City for isotonic facelifting. Most women over 40 are now aware of the importance of taking calcium to prevent this disease, which causes a softening of the bones. In addition, during these and other related experiments, researchers noticed several collateral benefits that followed bioelectrical treatment: nerve regeneration, healing of new and/or chronic wounds, healing of soft tissue, healing of muscle, and sterilization of wounds.

I have given you this background to illustrate the potential value of the Ionic Bath Machine as a healing tool. I think it is the kind of appliance that no home should be without. I hope in the future it will be readily available to everyone at a reasonable cost. Presently, it is primarily used in salons and clinics. The best thing to do is to call your local salons and inquire as to whether or not they use the PDG machines, and whether the machine would be helpful to you. Further information can be obtained through Alice Braunstein, owner of the Images Salon in San Rafael, California. She has worked with several types of these machines and would be able to help you find out more about this type of treatment. She can be reached at 415-457-1154.

SALON TREATMENTS

There are several types of cellulite treatments offered by salons. I have broken down the different types into three categories: wraps, massages, and machines. Most are sold in a series of ten or more treatments because it takes that long to begin to see results. Remember that treatments of this type may not be successful without some weight loss, and that also takes time.

Wraps   The salon wrap treatment usually consists of three to five steps:

Step 1. Exfoliation by brushing, loofah, cream, or seaweed.

Step 2. Wrapping in either an herbal mixture, seaweed, or a special cream.

Step 3. Massage (optional).

Step 4. Application of body lotion or cream.

Step 5. Using a passive muscle machine at different times during treatment (optional).

Wraps alone are not an effective cellulite treatment. However, they work well when used in conjunction with diet modification, weight loss, and exercise. The effectiveness of a wrap treatment depends on the quality of both the products used and the massage. The small amount of research available on this type of treatment seems to indicate that the most effective products contain seaweed. However, since seaweed treatments are so new to this country, it will take time to properly evaluate their benefits.

Massage   There are two types of massage used specifically for cellulite: lymphatic drainage and deep tissue. Lymphatic drainage is a gentle massage, while deep tissue work is painful and can even cause bruising. However, both are equally necessary. Lymphatic drainage helps to unblock lymph to prevent the further accumulation of toxins. Deep tissue massage helps to break up hard pockets of accumulated fat and toxins—this increases circulation to blocked areas.

Machines   By passively exercising the muscles, cellulite treatment machines act on cellulite in two ways: First, they improve the muscle tone, which helps the muscles to release toxins, and second, they work to help break up fat deposits and increase circulation.

Although there are many different makes of cellulite treatment machines, they all fall into one of two categories: those with electrode pads and those with electrode probes which are used to manually manipulate the muscles. Nemectron, a German company founded by medical researcher Dr. Nemec, makes one of the most widely used pad-type machines. The probe type is newer and less widely used, but is considered to be more effective for increasing muscle tone.

The Anushka Institute in New York City offers one of the most effective cellulite treatments available. It is based on a program developed by medical doctors in Switzerland, where such treatments are considered to be a part of physical therapy and are paid for by socialized medicine. The Anushka program combines Nemectron machine treatments—which take place two or three times a week—with diet modification, at-home treatment products, wraps, and massage. In between treatments, the client is instructed to use a soap containing crushed seaweed, algae, and kelp, along with a sisal brush or mitt to stimulate the "problematic areas." This is then followed by the application of a gel that stimulates circulation. The gel contains high concentrations of rosemary oil and chlorophyll, which makes it similar to those discussed earlier in the aromatherapy treatment of cellulite.

The photographs shown here were taken over a 5-week period and are unretouched. The client states that after eight sessions she had lost 5 pounds, 1 ½ inches off both thighs, 1 inch off both knees, and 1 inch off her hips. She modified her diet only slightly, by reducing the number of fats, and adding more water, and, she tried to eat proteins, carbohydrates, and fruits separately from each other (as recommended by Anushka). She also cut down on desserts, used sugarless products, and ate more salads. She increased her exercise regimen with 20 minutes of stretching and muscle conditioning every morning.

Buttocks and thighs before cellulite treatment (Anushka Institute, New York)

Buttocks and thighs after cellulite treatment (Anushka Institute, New York)

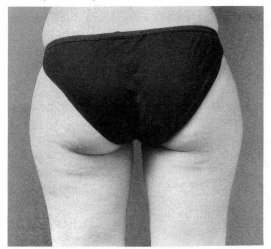

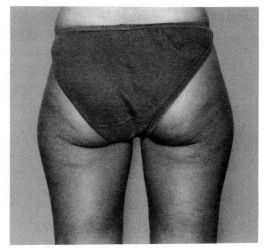

67

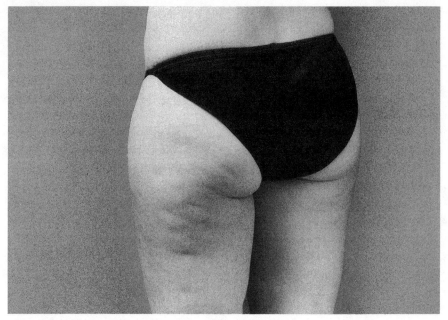

Outer thighs before cellulite treatment (Anushka Institute, New York)

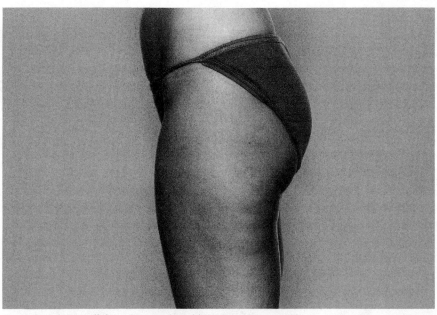

Outer thighs after cellulite treatment (Anushka Institute, New York)

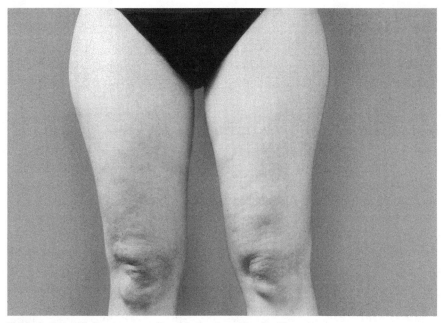

Thighs before cellulite treatment (Anushka Institute, New York)

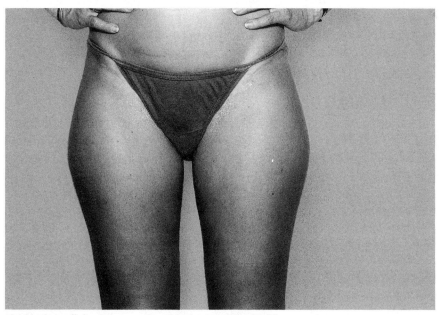

Thighs after cellulite treatment (Anushka Institute, New York)

The Anushka salon offers a special maintenance program of eight treatments that may be spread out over a few months, as needed. The client we sent was so satisfied that she will continue to use these treatments as well as maintain her new exercise routine and good eating habits. The Anushka Institute is located at 241 East 60th Street, New York City, 212-355-6404.

How Diet Affects Cellulite

If we work on the assumption that cellulite is caused, in part, by a combination of toxins, fat, and water retention, we can create nutritional guidelines to treat these problems. The most nutritious diet is low in salt and fat and consists mainly of fresh, unprocessed foods. White sugar, caffeine (in all forms, including headache medications, soda, coffee, and black tea), and nicotine should be eliminated. The latter two encourage development of cellulite because they impede circulation and deplete your body of cell-building nutrients and oxygen. Alcohol should be eliminated or at least kept to the minimums described in Chapter 2. You can use the following sample menus to help get you started on the anticellulite way of eating. You'll be surprised at how easy and delicious eating right can be, and you'll love the way you look and feel. Before starting, it's important to note that your diet must include the equivalent of 2 tablespoons of cold-pressed, natural vegetable oil per day. This is necessary to maintain healthy hair, skin, and the body's natural lubrication system.

The Anticellulite Way of Eating

Breakfast Foods

Whole grain, low-salt cereals (such as Nabisco Shredded Wheat and Quaker Puffed Wheat or Rice), topped with low-fat or nonfat milk

Fresh fruit, plain or with 2 tablespoons of plain or vanilla yogurt

Whole grain toast spread with natural apple butter and 1 tablespoon low-fat cottage cheese or farmer cheese

Open-faced grilled cheese made with fat-free soya cheese and whole grain bread.

Cream of Wheat or oatmeal with raisins and cinnamon, with a little honey for sweetener

Scrambled eggs made with two egg whites and one yolk (once a week), with whole-grain toast or Wasa bread

2 tablespoons sugar-, salt-, and oil-free granola, ½ cup white grapes, and 2
    tablespoons plain or vanilla yogurt
Fresh carrot or orange juice (8 ounces) may accompany any breakfast.

Lunch The best selections for lunch are salads that contain a wide variety
of vegetables. Choose small quantities of several of the following raw
vegetables—cucumber, tomato, lettuce, spinach, endive, watercress, sprouts,
cabbage, carrots, mushrooms, radish, peppers, snow peas, green peas,
onion, celery, fennel—and fruits—apple, pear, orange, pineapple, banana,
raisins, figs, peaches, grapes, and grapefruit. The variety available will allow
you to create many interesting combinations.

When I steam vegetables for dinner, I make enough to have leftovers
for lunch. This is a convenient way to have a good selection on hand when
you want it. The following vegetables are delicious when served cold
with a squeeze of lemon juice or added to a salad: corn, brussels sprouts,
asparagus, artichokes, snow peas, green peas, string beans, beets, onions,
carrots, zucchini, yellow squash, lima beans, and potatoes. Potatoes are an
especially good addition to cold chicken or fish salads, as they are filling
and satisfying but free of fat and low in calories. Grains such as rice, kasha,
lentils, and couscous are also good additions to any salad.

Dried or fresh herbs add dimension to salads and cold vegetables.
Three of the most versatile are tarragon, basil, and dill, though I don't
recommend using them together. Cilantro is an excellent addition, but
should only be used fresh as it loses its flavor when it is dried. Curry or
nutmeg make excellent additions to chicken, turkey, tuna, or shrimp salads.

The following are some of my favorite recipes. The fresher the
ingredients, the better they will taste. Feel free to substitute your favorite
nuts, seeds, or spices in place of the ones I suggest. However, keep in mind
that nuts and some seeds are high in natural oil and should be used
sparingly. Also, feel free to vary the amounts of ingredients, bearing in
mind that those containing oil or fat are the ones that should be kept to a
minimum.

SPINACH SALAD

2 cups fresh spinach leaves   *½ to 1 whole orange, in sections*
1 teaspoon chopped pine nuts   *2 to 3 mushrooms, sliced*

DRESSING
  Fresh lemon juice to taste   *1 teaspoon olive oil*

First mix dressing, then toss with salad ingredients.

FARMER SALAD

1 ripe, medium-sized tomato,
    sliced
3-inch section of peeled cucumber,
    sliced
2 to 3 radishes, sliced
2 tablespoons low-fat cottage
    cheese or farmer cheese

1 tablespoon sour half-and-half or
    low-fat yogurt
1 to 2 green onions, chopped
    (optional)
    Fresh cracked pepper to taste
    (optional)
    Natural spice mixture such as
    Spike, to taste (optional)

Mix all ingredients together in a bowl.

MIXED FRUIT SALAD

1 handful of red grapes
1 apple, diced
1/2 stalk celery, diced
1 tablespoon raisins

2 walnuts, chopped
2 tablespoons low-fat vanilla yogurt
1 cup shredded lettuce

Mix together all ingredients except lettuce. Spread the lettuce on a dinner plate and place the mixture on top.

ISRAELI SALAD

1 ripe tomato, diced
3-inch section of peeled cucumber,
    sliced

1/2 green pepper, chopped
1 teaspoon finely chopped red
    onion

DRESSING
    Lemon juice and freshly ground pepper to taste.

Mix dressing; toss with salad ingredients.

SHREDDED CARROT AND APPLE SALAD

1 carrot, shredded
1 apple, shredded or diced
1/2 cup pineapple chunks (fresh
    or packed in water)
1 tablespoon raisins

2 walnuts, chopped
2 tablespoons of any flavor of
    yogurt
1 cup shredded lettuce or spinach

Mix all ingredients together in a bowl, except for lettuce. Place the lettuce on a dinner plate and place mixture on top.

ORANGE AND PEAR SALAD

1 orange, sectioned
1 pear, diced

2 tablespoons low-fat vanilla yogurt
1 cup shredded lettuce or spinach

Mix together the first three ingredients and place on top of shredded lettuce.

CANNED SALMON OR TUNA SALAD

1 3½-ounce can salmon or
   tuna (packed in water)
½ stalk celery, diced
1 small green apple, diced
1 tablespoon safflower oil
   mayonnaise

1 teaspoon minced onion
   (optional)
Dried or fresh dill to taste
Lemon juice or vinegar to
   taste

Rinse the tuna or salmon in a strainer under cold, running water for one full minute. Drain well in the strainer by pressing on the fish with the back of a large spoon. Mix together with all of the remaining ingredients. This serves two and can be made into a sandwich or placed on top of shredded lettuce.

SARDINE SALAD

1 3½-ounce can sardines or
   herring
3-inch section of peeled cucumber,
   diced

1 slice whole-grain toast or 2 slices
   Wasa bread
Fresh lemon juice or vinegar
   to taste

Drain fish well and mix with other ingredients. This salad is also delicious topped with thin slices of sweet onion.

DICED COLD CHICKEN OR TURKEY

½ cup diced cooked chicken or
   turkey

1 medium tomato, diced
1 tablespoon fresh cilantro

DRESSING
½ teaspoon sesame oil

Lemon juice to taste

Mix dressing, then toss with other ingredients. This salad may be eaten as is, in a sandwich, on Wasa bread, or on shredded lettuce.

If you roast a whole chicken or small turkey, you can eat it in a variety of ways for days. Cold, sliced fowl is delicious served as an open-faced sandwich on whole-grain bread that has been spread with mustard.

POTATO AND TUNA SALAD

½ of a 3½-ounce can of tuna rinsed well
½ cup diced cooked potatoes
¼ cup diced celery
¼ cup diced cucumber
1 tablespoon safflower oil mayonnaise

½ teaspoon dried dill or tarragon
1 cup shredded lettuce
Fresh lemon juice to taste
Freshly cracked pepper to taste

Mix together all ingredients except lettuce and serve on a dinner plate on which the lettuce has been spread. If you wish, add tomato slices or cherry tomatoes.

DICED COLD SHRIMP SALAD

½ cup shrimp, cooked and chilled
¼ cup diced celery
1 teaspoon safflower oil mayonnaise or whipped cream cheese

1 cup chopped lettuce
1 teaspoon minced green onions (optional)
Lemon juice to taste

Mix all ingredients together. Dried dill or tarragon can be added to create different flavors.

COLD FISH SALAD

½ cup diced fish, cooked and chilled
¼ cup diced celery or fennel
¼ cup diced cucumber or radish

1 ripe medium tomato, cored and seeded
1 teaspoon finely chopped sweet onion (optional)

DRESSING
1 teaspoon safflower oil mayonnaise

½ teaspoon fresh or dried herbs
Lemon juice or vinegar to taste

Mix dressing separately, then toss with other ingredients. This salad can be made from any type of leftover fish. I often broil or grill an extra piece of shark, swordfish, salmon, or sea bass at dinner so that I can have it in a salad for the next day's lunch.

Any of the above salads may be sprinkled with a tablespoon of wheat germ for added protein and eaten with one or two pieces of Wasa bread.

LETTUCE, TOMATO, AND CUCUMBER SANDWICH

1 teaspoon mustard
½ teaspoon safflower oil
    mayonnaise
2 slices whole-grain bread
4 slices ripe tomato

2-inch section of peeled cucumber,
    sliced
2 lettuce leaves
    Freshly ground pepper

Mix mustard with mayonnaise. Spread on bread. Layer tomatoes, cucumber, and lettuce on mustard/mayonnaise mixture and add a dash of pepper for taste.

COLD CHICKEN OR TURKEY SANDWICH

1 teaspoon mustard and/or ½
    teaspoon safflower oil
    mayonnaise
1 or 2 slices whole-grain bread
4 slices cold chicken or turkey

2 slices ripe tomato
2 leaves of lettuce or spinach
    (2 fresh basil leaves added to
    this sandwich give it an extra
    good flavor)

Spread mustard and/or mayonnaise on bread. Stack chicken/turkey, tomato, lettuce/spinach, and basil leaves.

CHICKEN BURGERS

¼ to ½ pound ground,
    uncooked chicken (or turkey)
    Bread crumbs to coat

½ teaspoon finely chopped
    onion (optional)

Select chicken breasts and ask the butcher to remove all skin and fat before grinding them to the same consistency as hamburger. Preheat oven to 350°F. Form ground chicken into patties and coat with bread crumbs. Bake for 15 to 20 minutes. Serve as you would hamburgers, with pasta, vegetables, or a salad.

HOT OR COLD POACHED FISH

Fish of your choice
    (instructions for poaching are
    on p. 77)

Dry white wine to cover (or
    water and wine may be mixed)
Herbs (for added flavor)

Preheat oven to 350°F. Add herbs appropriate to the fish you are cooking to the poaching liquid for flavor. Place fish in a poaching pan in the oven until done. Serve fish with a side of steamed vegetables or in a sandwich.

The following sauce is a delicious, low-fat addition to any poached fish:

SAUCE

2 teaspoons plain yogurt   *Squeeze of fresh lemon juice*
1/2 teaspoon mustard
1/4 teaspoon dried or fresh dill or
*   tarragon*

Mix all ingredients together and spread over fish, or on bread, if making a sandwich.

Dinner A basic anticellulite dinner should include the following: broiled, baked, or poached fish, shellfish, veal, chicken, or turkey; steamed vegetables or a raw vegetable salad; and pasta or a steamed whole grain such as brown rice, bulgar wheat, or couscous. Try substituting ground chicken or turkey in place of ground beef in burgers, meat sauce, meat loaf, and chili. If you choose potato for a vegetable, top it with freshly ground pepper, 1 teaspoon plain yogurt, and some chopped chives or steamed leeks. Don't use margarine or butter on vegetables; instead, squeeze a bit of fresh lemon juice on them and sprinkle with dry or fresh herbs and pepper.

Here are some easy, low-fat sauces that cook in minutes and may be spooned over fish, veal, or fowl that has been broiled, baked, or poached:

WHITE WINE AND SHALLOT SAUCE

1 teaspoon margarine
Few drops of olive oil
2 large shallots, finely chopped
1/2 cup dry white wine

Melt the margarine and olive oil in a nonstick frying pan. Sauté the shallots for 1 minute. Add the dry white wine and cook over high heat until it is reduced to half (about 5 minutes). Pour over fish, veal, or chicken.

For another variation of this, add finely chopped mushrooms at the same time as the shallots. If you crave a thicker sauce, add a dash of flour after the wine has cooked down a little. Red wine may also be used in place of white for a heavier sauce.

FRESH TOMATO SAUCE

1 small onion, diced
4 green onions, chopped
4 cloves garlic, finely chopped
1 tablespoon olive oil
5 very ripe, medium tomatoes,
*   coarsely chopped*
¼ cup water

1 teaspoon dried basil or 2
*   teaspoons chopped, fresh basil*
¼ teaspoon dried oregano or ½
*   teaspoon chopped, fresh*
*   oregano*
Pinch of thyme

In a nonstick frying pan, sauté the onions and two of the garlic cloves in the olive oil for 3 minutes. Add the tomatoes and water. Cook uncovered over medium-high heat for 10 minutes, then add the rest of the garlic, basil, oregano, and thyme. Cook for 8 to 10 minutes more.

To make a spicy version of this sauce, add crushed chili pepper to taste. This sauce is also delicious on pasta.

MARSALA SAUCE

2 large shallots, chopped
1 teaspoon margarine
Few drops of olive oil
¾ cup mushrooms, thinly sliced

⅓ cup dry Marsala wine
⅓ cup chicken broth (low-salt
*   broth, consommé or boullion)*

Sauté shallots in margarine and olive oil in a nonstick frying pan for 1 minute. Add the mushrooms and cook for another minute or two. Add Marsala wine and chicken broth. Cook over medium-high heat for a few minutes until reduced to half. Pour over veal, chicken, or fish.

When preparing fish I suggest you poach it. This is one of the easiest and most delicious recipes I've ever used.

POACHING LIQUID

Equal amounts water and dry
*   white wine to cover fish*
⅓ cup shallots, finely chopped

⅓ cup mushrooms, finely
*   chopped*
⅓ cup parsley, finely chopped

This poaching liquid also may be reduced after poaching to make a sauce: Pour water and wine into the bottom of a poaching pan. Add shallots, mushrooms, and fresh parsley. Place fish on the poaching rack and cook at 350° until done. If you do not own a poaching pan, place the fish in a large skillet with enough poaching liquid to barely cover it and seal with a tight-fitting lid. Cook over medium heat until tender. Remove the fish and keep it warm. Pour the poaching mixture into a saucepan and cook over high heat until reduced by half. Pour over fish and serve. If you can afford a few extra calories, add a small amount of half and half to the reduced poaching mixture to make a light cream sauce. Cook this until it begins to thicken.

For a change, once a week you may want to have something sautéed. Thinly sliced veal, veal chops, boneless chicken breasts, scallops, prawns, or fish steaks are all delicious when cooked in this manner: Quickly brown each side in a nonstick frying pan coated with 1 teaspoon safflower oil. Remove the meat or fish and add ¼ cup red or white wine, or sherry. Cook for 1 to 2 minutes, then return the meat to the pan and cook for a minute or two, until tender. Thinly sliced mushrooms and/or shallots may be added to this for 1 minute before the liquid is added.

If you crave red meat, by all means eat it for dinner once in a while. Just be sure to choose a lean cut and trim all visible fat before cooking. Broiling and grilling are the preferable methods of cooking because they add no fat.

Home-made soups are delicious and can be filling enough to be a complete meal when served with a hearty sourdough or whole-grain bread. If you have never made soups, you'll be surprised at how easy they are to create. I suggest you investigate different cookbooks for inventive ideas. The following are three of my favorite, original recipes:

SPLIT PEA AND ZUCCHINI SOUP

1 large onion, coarsely chopped
1 tablespoon olive or safflower oil
1 clove garlic, peeled and finely chopped
1 cup dried green or yellow peas
1 tablespoon dried dill or 2 tablespoons fresh, chopped dill

4 cups cold water
3 large carrots, sliced
3 medium zucchinis, sliced ½-inch thick
½ cup low-fat or skim milk
A small dollop of sour half and half as garnish

Sauté onions in oil until they become transparent. Add garlic and sauté for 2 more minutes. Add split peas, carrots, dill, and water. Cook, uncovered, on medium heat for 40 minutes. Add zucchinis and cook for 15 minutes or until peas are soft. Remove from heat and add milk. Blend in food processor or blender until smooth. Serve in bowls and top with 1 tablespoon sour half and half and freshly ground pepper.

ONION AND CARROT SOUP

5 large onions, sliced ½ inch
thick
2 tablespoons margarine
1 teaspoon honey
2 tablespoons flour
2 cups beef broth

2 cups chicken broth
1 cup water
½ teaspoon dried thyme
3 medium carrots, sliced ½ inch
thick
Parmesan cheese for garnish

Sauté onions in margarine over low heat for 20 minutes. Add honey and flour, and brown for 5 minutes. Add broth and water. (If you are a vegetarian, you may substitute vegetable broth.) Add carrots and thyme. Simmer uncovered for 30 minutes, then cover and remove from heat. Let the soup cool for an hour or more, then reheat and serve with sourdough or French bread. Sprinkle Parmesan cheese on top before serving.

NANNIE'S CHICKEN SOUP

1 whole chicken cut into large
pieces, including neck and
giblets but not liver
2 large stalks celery, cut in half
3 large carrots, cut in half
1 large turnip, quartered

1 large onion, quartered
1 bay leaf
2 whole garlic cloves, peeled
6 peppercorns
Handful of parsley

This is the easiest soup of all. Place all ingredients into a large, heavy pot and bring to a boil. Lower heat to medium and cook uncovered for 2 hours. Skim the fat off the top with a large spoon as it appears. Remove pot from heat, cover and refrigerate. Allow the soup to cool and congeal completely so that the fat forms a hard layer on the top. Before reheating, remove the layer of fat. Pick out the pieces of carrot, take the chicken meat off the bone, and set aside. Strain the soup, add the pieces of carrot and chicken, reheat and serve. This soup is delicious served with egg noodles, rice, or diced potatoes.

Vegetable soup is an easy soup to make and a good way to use up odds and ends of assorted vegetables. It can be made by using any combination of chopped vegetables and water. Use a 3 to 1 proportion of water to vegetables and add the fast-cooking vegetables toward the end of cooking. Any type of soup stock, such as chicken, beef, or fish, may be used in place of or in addition to water. Try experimenting with different herbs to create various flavors. When making vegetable soup keep the following in mind: If potatoes are added, they will cause the soup to thicken. Beans or rice may be added but should be cooked separately to avoid making the soup too starchy.

You may drink as much herb tea, sodium-free mineral water or seltzer, water-processed decaffeinated coffee, and fresh fruit juice as you like. However, do not add any sugar or artificial sweetener; use honey instead if you must have sweetener. Try to drink eight glasses of liquid a day. A glass of wine with dinner or a cocktail beforehand is fine, but when it comes to calories, the less alcohol the better.

Remember, this is not a diet, but a way of eating. Once you begin to see results you can occasionally add hamburgers, pizza, or other high-fat meals. For further inspiration and information on low-fat eating and recipes, I recommend the following books:

Jane Brody's Good Food Book, by Jane Brody. Bantam Books, 1987

The New American Diet: The Lifetime Family Eating Plan for Good Health, by Sonja L. Connor, M.S., R.D., and William E. Connor, M.D. Simon and Schuster, 1986

Deliciously Simple, by Harriet Roth. New American Library, 1986

The New Laurel's Kitchen, by Laurel Robertson, Carol Flinders, and Brian Ruppenthal. Ten Speed Press, 1986

Seafood: A Collection of Heart-Healthy Recipes, by Janis Harsila, R.D., and Evie Hansen. Natural Seafood Educators, 1986. Available in bookstores and sold by mail order. Send $11.95 plus $2 shipping and handling charges to National Seafood Educators, P.O. Box 60006, Richmond Beach, WA 98160.

The Great American Seafood Cookbook: From Sea to Shining Sea, by Susan Herrmann Loomis. Workman, 1988.

Spot Exercises That Really Work

Although this section is concerned with specific types of exercise for specific problems, these should be integrated with a regular aerobic exercise program. Aerobic exercise, which raises your heart rate and increases your intake of oxygen, is not only beneficial to the shape of your body, but also good for your skin. Vigorous aerobic exercise revs up circulation as well as stimulating oil- and sweat-gland production, both of which help your body rid itself of toxins and combat the "slowdown" of aging skin.

The increased intake of oxygen also helps in the production of new cells. One of the greatest benefits of aerobic exercise may be the boost it gives to collagen and elastin production. These are the fibers responsible for youthful skin because they strengthen the skin's connective tissue and help it maintain its natural elasticity. Here is a list that will give you an idea of the wide range of exercises that are considered to be aerobic: dancing, Jazzercise, aerobic or low-impact aerobic classes, circuit weight training, running, race walking, bouncing on a trampoline, tennis, racquetball, squash, swimming, bicycling, and walking at a fast pace. Whatever type of exercise you choose should be done a minimum of three times per week for a period of 20 minutes followed by a slow, "cool down" time of 10 minutes. Of course, daily aerobic exercise, if it can be managed, is optimal.

ISOMETRICS

The classic form of spot exercise is called isometrics. In this type of exercise, a muscle is isolated, tightened, then moved very slightly to cause contraction and relaxation. The actual movement is almost imperceptible, unlike other types of exercises that are made up of large, vigorous movements. An isometric exercise program is designed to augment, rather than replace, a regular aerobic exercise program because it does not provide cardiovascular fitness.

Although cellulite must be treated in all the various ways described earlier, isometrics works very fast to lift sagging behinds, stomachs, and thighs. In fact, very often lumps and bumps on buttocks, stomach, and thighs may be the result of slackened muscles, rather than fat. Tightening the muscles that support these areas can actually make cellulite disappear.

CALLANETICS

This has been demonstrated most successfully by ex-dancer and exercise expert Callan Pinckney. In her best-selling book and videotape, *Callanetics: Ten Years Younger in Ten Hours* (Morrow, 1984), Ms. Pinckney combines isometrics with dance stretches and yoga principles into a program called Callanetics. The unretouched before and after photographs in her book illustrate the progress made by several of her students. These are the most impressive I have ever seen. This is due partly to the fact that the program works in a matter of days, rather than months. Callanetics is the exercise program for those who are programmed to expect immediate results. It is almost too good to be true, but it is. To help illustrate my enthusiasm over Callanetics, William Morrow and Company has graciously allowed me to reprint a series of before and after photographs of Ms. Pinckney's student

Jean. The photographs are certified unretouched and were taken over a period of 9 weeks. Jean exercised twice a week for 1 hour during that period and lost a total of 5 pounds. The miraculous changes are caused by a tightening and lifting of the muscles that support the buttocks, abdomen, and thighs.

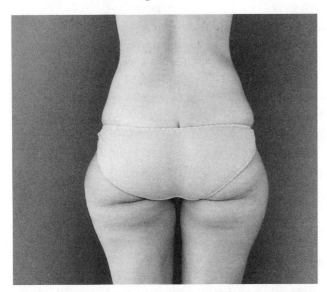

Before Callanetics treatments begin

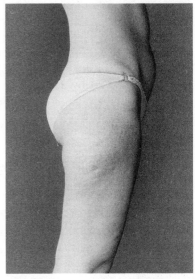

Before Callanetics treatments begin

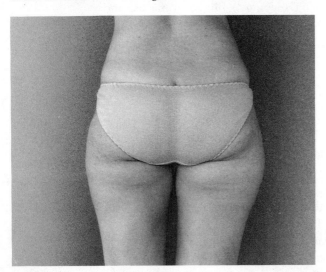

After 13 one-hour Callanetics sessions

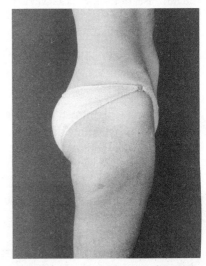

After 13 one-hour Callanetics sessions

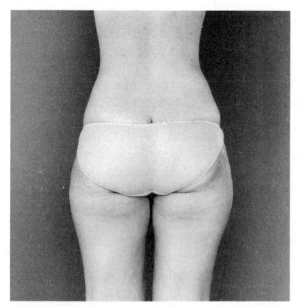

After 17 one-hour Callanetics sessions

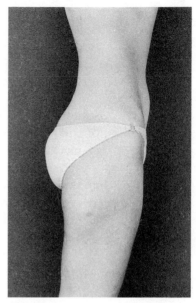

After 17 one-hour Callanetics sessions

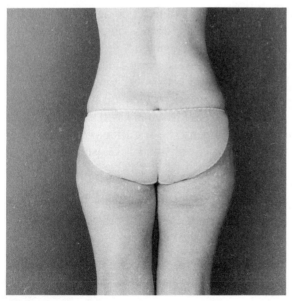

After 19 one-hour Callanetics sessions

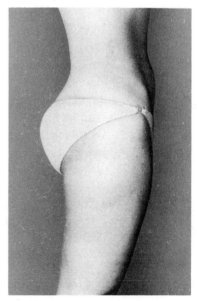

After 19 one-hour Callanetics sessions

Ms. Pinckney told me that most people have to exercise only for 10 hours before seeing miraculous results. In spite of the extremity of Jean's case, had she done four more sessions, every last vestige of her remaining "goosh" would have disappeared. Unfortunately, deadlines for the publication of Ms. Pinckney's book prevented the inclusion of the final results.

In my personal testing of this program, I saw visible results after two sessions, the most noticeable being a disappearance of the dimpled areas of skin beneath and on the sides of my buttocks. A real change in the shape of my buttocks and thighs was noticeable after five sessions. Continual practice of the exercises, on a daily basis, for 1 week made an enormous improvement. The only area left with a small amount of dimpling was in the center of my buttocks. I expect that when I lose the two remaining extra pounds I'm still carrying, that will disappear. I now do the series of exercises, which takes about 40 minutes, twice a week, as recommended by Ms. Pinckney. I do some form of aerobic exercise (bicycling, low-impact aerobic exercise class, Nautilus machines, tennis, race walking) on other days.

Because we can trace the cause of cellulite to a number of conditions, it is important to remember that a successful cellulite treatment must consist of a total program.

As I suggested earlier, an effective cellulite-reducing or elimination program must encompass exercise to increase circulation and a proper diet and detoxification to reduce the number of toxins in the body. Detoxification can be achieved through the use of seaweed baths, nutritional supplements, diuretic teas, drinking six to eight glasses of water daily, and by modifying your diet. Good, effective methods to increase your circulation can include everything from salon machine treatments and dry brushing to aerobic and isometric exercises. Remember to be suspicious of any home or salon treatment that promises "instant" results and isn't used in conjunction with a diet and exercise program.

Keep in mind that cellulite treatment takes time. Your body didn't acquire those lumps and bumps overnight and they won't disappear that way. But I promise that with the faithful and continued practice of the good habits discussed here you will eventually see visible and significant results.

C H A P T E R
SEVEN

BREAST
TREATMENTS

There are a variety of complaints that women may have about their breasts: too big, too small, too droopy, uneven size, stretch marks, and misplaced nipples. Even if you began life with perfect breasts, time, gravity, and childbearing would eventually change them. For this reason, the most common complaint women have about their breasts is the loss of firmness that comes with age. The skin loses its elasticity as gravity begins to pull the breasts downward. This is a problem that may be somewhat improved without surgery by strengthening the breast support system. Surgical procedures that handle other breast problems will be discussed later in the chapter.

Understanding the Breast Support System

Since the breasts themselves do not contain any muscle, they cannot be exercised into shape like other parts of the body. There are, however, two ways to help restore firmness to the breasts. One is to maintain or improve the supportive skin's elasticity; the other is to exercise and strengthen the pectoral muscles. The treatments discussed throughout this chapter are geared to either improve the elasticity of the skin or strengthen the supporting muscles. The pectoral muscles, which lie beneath the breasts, may be toned by proper exercise. Once the pectorals become stronger, they help to support the breasts and counteract sagging.

The skin that surrounds the breasts may be toned by isometric exercise, which, in turn, helps to support the breasts. Applying a good moisturizer after bathing will help to keep the skin soft. It is also important to remember to protect this skin by applying a sun block on the neck and chest (and breasts if they are to be exposed) while in the sun. Wearing a bra, on a daily basis, helps to counteract the force of gravity and prevent tearing delicate breast tissue. It is especially important to wear a supportive bra while exercising. There are several different styles of "sport bras" on the market. Their basic function is to hold the breasts close to the body, which keeps them from bouncing. It is the bouncing action that stretches the skin surrounding the breasts and tears the supportive tissue.

Supportive Muscle Exercises

The following exercises help to firm and tone the pectoral muscles. You may incorporate them into your regular exercise routine or do them separately. To get the fastest results, I recommend doing them twice a day for 2 to 3 weeks. You may then cut down to once a day for 2 to 3 weeks, and after that time to three times a week. If you stop the exercises and your breasts begin to sag again, you should start the program over from the beginning.

The only equipment needed to perform these exercises are two 3-pound weights. These may be purchased in a sporting goods store either as mini-barbells or hand weights, or improvised by using a 3-pound jar of anything (peanut butter, jam) or cans of paint.

1. Lie on your back, with your knees bent and your feet on the floor, holding a weight in each hand. Hold your arms straight up, perpendicular to the floor. Slowly extend your arms out to the sides, lowering them to the floor; then slowly raise them back up to their original position. Repeat 10 times. Increase repetitions by 2 or 3 each day until you can do 30.
2. Sit on the floor with your back straight, your legs either out straight or comfortably crossed, and your arms stretched out in front of you. Hold a

weight in each hand with one fist over the other. Slowly open your arms to the width of your shoulders, then bring your hands back to their original position. Alternate right hand over left for 10 repetitions, gradually working up to 30.

3. Lie on your back on the floor with your arms straight up (perpendicular to the floor), knees bent, and feet on the floor, and a weight in each hand. Keeping your arms parallel, slowly lower them over your head to the floor. Slowly return your arms to their original position and repeat 10 times, gradually increasing to 30.

4. Sit on the floor with legs either out in front of you or comfortably crossed, a weight in each hand, palms toward the ceiling, and your arms outstretched in front of you. Open your arms slowly to the sides (not farther back than your shoulders). Slowly return your arms to their original position and repeat 10 times, eventually working up to 30.

Do the following exercises after completing the above series, to strengthen the skin and muscles above the breasts:

1. Sitting or standing comfortably, place your hands together in front of your body in a prayer position with your elbows out and at the height of your shoulders. Press your palms together as hard as you can and hold for 5 seconds; then slowly release to the count of 5 and repeat 20 times. Gradually increase to 50.

2. Sit cross-legged on the floor with your back straight and your hands clasped behind your neck with your elbows out. Inhale slowly and deeply through your nose to the count of 5, then exhale to the count of 5. Repeat 10 times.

3. Sit comfortably in a straight-back chair and slowly lean your head back to look up at the ceiling. Open your mouth; then, to the count of 5, bring your lower jaw up until your upper teeth rest inside the lower ones. Hold this position while you inhale and exhale through your nose to the count of 5. Then slowly release the lower jaw to the count of 5, and slowly bring your head back to the starting position. Repeat the entire exercise two more times.

Be aware that isometric exercises do not work overnight. Allow 3 weeks before you expect to see any results. But plan on doing the exercises for several months before making any real judgment as to their effectiveness.

At-Home Treatments

Over the past year, I have diligently tested almost every "bust treatment" presently available on the American market. This includes bust creams, masks, tonics, lotions, ampoules, and appliances. Despite the incredible claims of renewed firmness and youthfulness made by the companies that manufacture these products, I am sorry to report that none of them made the slightest bit of difference to the naked eye. The creams, masks, lotions, tonics, and contents of the ampoules felt good on the skin, smelled good, and helped to make the skin soft and smooth; but any good moisturizing lotion would have done the same. If you want to pamper yourself with an expensive product to use on your bust, by all means do so, as long as you realize that it will not perform any miracles.

The only bust appliance available in this country, the Clarins Model Bust hydro-therapeutic appliance, cannot affect the firmness of the breasts in any way since there are no muscles to be either strengthened or pumped up. Clarins describes the appliance as "the ideal bust-massage appliance which, by simply attaching it to the cold water tap at home, allows an effective beauty treatment for the bust and décolleté." I am sure that the swirling cold water would momentarily have a tightening effect on the skin (as any cold water does), but this can in no way repair sagging breasts.

Salon Treatments

Many salons now offer a variety of treatments, such as masks and ampoules containing active plant extracts, that promise to firm and tighten the bust. However, like the at-home treatments, most of these do little more than provide relaxation and soften the skin.

If you have neglected your skin or are seeing the results of overexposure to the sun, a bust treatment, like a facial, will give good results *as far as improving the look of your skin*. Most bust masks or treatments of this type begin with the application of an exfoliant. When this is removed, the dead layer of cells comes off as well, leaving the skin smooth and soft. Then the contents of an ampoule, an oil, or bust cream is applied and massaged into the skin. These work to soften and plump the skin so that lines or sun damage are less evident. Sometimes a light steam or warm cloth wrap is used to help these products penetrate. The final step of most bust treatments is the application of a mask, usually mud or paraffin based. These are designed to firm and tighten the skin, but you must realize that the effects are temporary, lasting only for several hours.

Like any good salon treatment, one designed for the bust can be a wonderful experience. I only caution you to remember that this type of treatment cannot restore muscle tone, lift, erase stretch marks, or increase the size of the breasts. It may be a nice thing to treat yourself to during the summer season when skin is exposed, or prior to an evening when you're going to be wearing a low-cut dress.

NONSURGICAL LIFTS BY MACHINE

The most effective type of salon treatment is one that employs electrodermal stimulation, electricity used to stimulate the muscles that lie beneath the skin. For this treatment, one of a number of machines designed to emit different types of mild electrical current is used. One of the best of these was designed by Paul Donat Groux, the same man who pioneered the Ionic Bath Machine. Call the salons in your area to find one that uses this type of machine to lift and firm the breasts and discuss the treatment with the salon managers to determine if it is right for you.

ACUPUNCTURE BREAST LIFT

For centuries the Chinese have been using acupuncture for the treatment of everything from facial rejuvenation to the curing of disease. Many modern acupuncture practitioners have adapted the treatment to fulfill their patients' desires for better or bigger breasts. The acupuncture breast lift takes approximately twenty 40-minute treatments over a period of 10 weeks. Each treatment costs between $25 and $50, making the total cost of the full treatment between $500 and $1,000. Once results are attained, one to two follow-up treatments per month are recommended. This is an expensive treatment that would eventually cost more than a surgical breast lift. Although several doctors claim to have performed this acupuncture operation satisfactorily, none were able to supply me with before and after photographs.

ACUPUNCTURE BREAST AUGMENTATION

Treatments for breast enlargement or augmentation are similar to those used for the breast lift, and the costs are approximately the same. Once desired results are attained, follow-up treatments are needed once or twice a month. Again, no doctors were able to supply me with before and after photos of this operation.

Since acupuncture is fast becoming a commonly practiced procedure in America, you should be able to find a reliable practitioner in your area. When interviewing practitioners, I recommend that you ask to see before and after photos or ask to contact one or two of their patients who have undergone the treatment. The success of the treatment will depend on the expertise of the practitioner. Although there are many acupuncturists, not all of them do breast treatments.

Surgical Treatments

BREAST AUGMENTATION

If you prefer instant and permanent reparation of diminutive breasts, your problem will be best solved surgically. New advances in breast augmentation surgery (augmentation mammaplasty) have made this a practical solution for many women. Unlike the old-fashioned implants, which were hard and inflexible, new flexible plastic sacks, or "envelopes," are filled with silicone gel and/or saline solution, which gives the breasts a softer, natural look and feel.

The classic operation is performed by making an incision either in the crease beneath the breast or around the lower border of the areola, the dark pink skin that surrounds the nipple. It is through one of these incisions that the envelope is inserted beneath the normal breast tissue, either in front of or behind the pectoral (chest) muscle. The incision is then closed. For many women, this operation causes a loss of feeling in the nipple that is sometimes permanent. For this reason, San Francisco plastic surgeon Dr. Robert Brink prefers an alternate procedure and makes an incision in the armpit—this eliminates the need to remove the nipple.

The operation is performed either in an office–surgical facility, under "twilight" anesthesia (local anesthesia and sedation) or in a hospital under general anesthesia. It takes approximately 2 hours. Although the patient may be able to move about freely within 48 hours, recovery time is usually between 1 and 2 weeks, depending on how fast the patient heals. Patients may not be able to participate in any vigorous activity for up to 8 weeks.

The before and after photos on pages 91 and 92 demonstrate this type of operation as performed by Dr. Robert Brink.

BREAST LIFT

An operation to lift sagging breasts but not increase their size may also be performed. The incisions for a surgical breast lift, or mastopexy, are the same as those used in a classic breast reduction, and leave an anchor-shaped scar from the nipple to the crease under the breast. The only difference between this procedure and a breast reduction is that very little tissue and skin are removed.

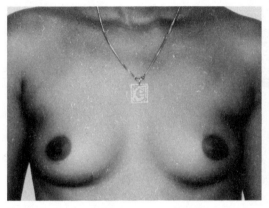
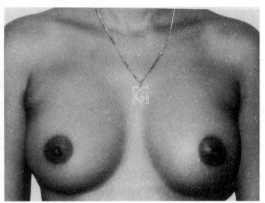

Breasts before augmentation surgery (Dr. Robert Brink)   Breasts after augmentation surgery (Dr. Robert Brink)

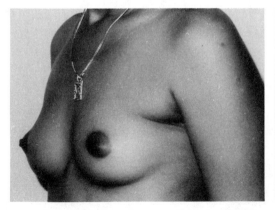
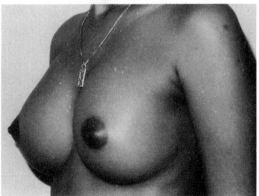

Breasts before augmentation surgery (Dr. Robert Brink)   Breasts after augmentation surgery (Dr. Robert Brink)

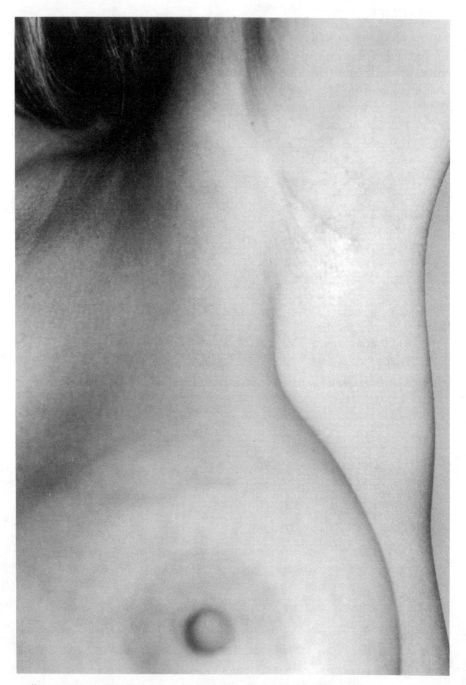

Axilla incision in armpit for breast augmentation surgery (Dr. Robert Brink)

BREAST REDUCTION

Breast reduction (reduction mammaplasty) is not as popular as breast augmentation, especially since curves and shapely figures are once again in fashion. But women who have overly large breasts may find them to be not only uncomfortable, but limiting. Most types of exercise, with the exception of swimming and weight lifting, cause the breasts to bounce. This can cause a strain on the muscles of the back and result in backaches, neckaches, and even headaches. For women whose excessively large breasts are not a result of being overweight, surgery may be the only answer.

The breast reduction technique most commonly practiced today in America is called brassiere pattern skin reduction. It involves making two incisions: a vertical keyhole-shaped incision around the nipple area and a half-moon-shaped incision following the contour of the breast that creates the new lower portion of the breast. Through these incisions, excess skin and fatty tissue are removed. In cases where the breasts may be so large that the nipples are misplaced, it may be necessary to move the nipples to where they are aesthetically correct. This, unfortunately, leads to loss of all sensitivity in the nipple area. However, Dr. Brink told me that it is not unusual for many women with oversized breasts to have little or no feeling in the nipple area anyway.

When the incision is closed, an anchor-shaped scar running from the nipple to the curve of the breast remains. Most of the lower portion of the scar is hidden in the fold of the breast and is not noticeable unless the breasts are lifted. However, the beginning of that scar may be visible in the cleavage portion of the breasts.

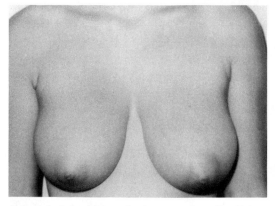

Breasts before classic reduction procedure (Dr. Robert Brink)

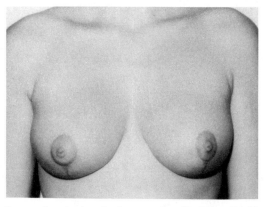

Breasts after classic reduction procedure (Dr. Robert Brink)

A new breast reduction technique, "Z-mammaplasty," has been developed in Europe and is just making its debut in this country. The new technique leaves minimal scarring and no scar whatsoever in the cleavage area. Dr. K. Ning Chang, M.D., a plastic and reconstructive surgeon with a practice in San Francisco, recently performed one of the first of these operations in this country. You may wish to ask your doctor about it.

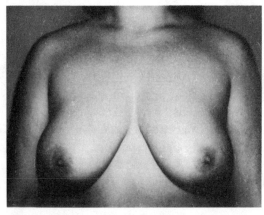

Breasts before "Z-mammaplasty" reduction technique (Dr. K. Ning Chang)

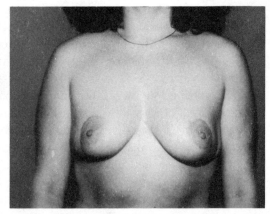

Breasts after "Z-mammaplasty" reduction technique (Dr. K. Ning Chang)

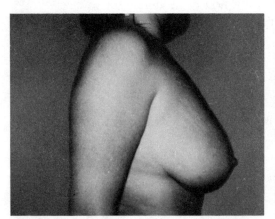

Breasts before "Z-mammaplasty" reduction technique (Dr. K. Ning Chang)

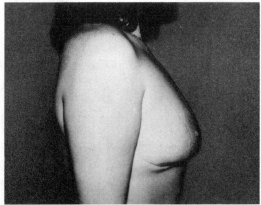

Breasts after "Z-mammaplasty" reduction technique (Dr. K. Ning Chang)

CHAPTER
EIGHT

THE NECK AND CHIN

The neck and chin are supported by part of the same major muscle system as the breasts. The fan-shaped platysma muscle extends from beneath the chin all the way down to the top of the chest. If you lean your head back and place your hand flat on the upper portion of your chest, then open your mouth slightly and slowly move your lower jaw up to meet your upper jaw, you will feel the pull of the platysma muscle. When this muscle becomes slack, as a result of age and with the pull of gravity, the skin on the neck loses its tautness and begins to sag. The chin, in turn, loses its definition or, if fat has accumulated, becomes "double." You can prevent much of this if you begin to exercise and tone the platysma muscle at an early age. Even if you don't begin until you're 35, you can make a great deal of improvement provided that your skin still has a good amount of elasticity. If your neck and chin have degenerated into a state of severe laxity, neither isometric exercise, nor acupressure, nor a nonsurgical lift will be sufficient to correct the condition. In cases such as this, cosmetic surgery may be required.

Isometric Exercises

Exercises 1 through 4 in Chapter 7 work to strengthen and tone the platysma muscle. These exercises also work well to help tighten and lift the chin and the skin of the neck.

The following exercise helps to strengthen the specific area of the platysma muscle where a double chin may form. To help make a double chin disappear, this exercise should be done twice a day (or more) for several weeks, or until progress is visible. At that point you may cut down to once a day. To prevent a double chin and help tighten the skin in that area, do the exercise only once a day. It's easy to do this almost anywhere, since it takes very little concentration and doesn't require the use of a mirror.

Sit or stand comfortably and open your mouth just enough to stick out your tongue. Stretch your tongue out as far as it will go, then attempt to touch the tip of your nose. Do this to the count of 5, then release to the count of 5. Close and relax your mouth for a few seconds, then repeat the exercise nine more times, making sure to close your mouth and relax your tongue in between each stretch.

At-Home Treatments

Like the bust treatments reviewed earlier, I am sorry to report that lotions, creams, ampoules, and masks are not effective regenerative treatments for a sagging neck and chin. Nor do I know of any preventive cosmetic treatment that's been proven effective. There are two different schools of thought regarding neck and skin treatment. Some say do nothing based on the theory that creams, lotions, or massage will have a softening effect that will eventually cause slackness. Proponents of the opposite theory believe that moisturization protects the skin on the neck and chin by preventing dryness and providing nourishment. I fall somewhere in between these two, believing that it is vital to keep the skin on the tight-dry side to help preserve its natural elasticity and tautness. Since rich, oil-based moisturizers have a softening effect on the skin, I recommend using an oil-free, gel moisturizer instead. It will provide nourishment and protection, but will also have a tightening effect on the skin. A light, natural, oil-based, vitamin-enriched moisturizer will also work well to provide nourishment, but will not have the beneficial tightening effect of a gel moisturizer. I recommend the use of products such as these, which contain vitamins and herbs, to help counteract the damaging effects of the environment. It is also very important to protect the neck and chin area with a sun block whenever you are going to be exposed to even a small amount of sunlight.

OIL-FREE GEL MOISTURIZERS

Aqualin (Light) Moisturizer	H, M*
Zia Cosmetics Gotu Kola Gel	M**

* For information about Aqualin, call 1-800-626-7888.
** For information about Zia Cosmetics, call 1-800-334-SKIN.

NATURAL OIL-BASED MOISTURIZERS

Chello Aloe Vera Day Cream*	H
Desert Essence Moisture Cream	H
Paul Penders Aloe Vera Day Cream*	H
Zia Cosmetics Everyday Moisturizer	M

* These appear to be the same product under different labels, as the ingredient listings are exactly the same.

There is a very effective, at-home treatment for the neck and chin; a mask that tightens and smooths this area temporarily. It has a powder base mixed in equal amounts with an aloe vera extract liquid, and is applied to the entire face and neck, extending down the chest as far as is necessary. When the mask dries and hardens, it has a "compacting" effect on the skin. Then it begins to pulse the neck and facial muscles, in much the same way as weight lifting pumps up muscles. When the muscles pump up, the skin covering them tightens and lines and wrinkles disappear. Even a double chin becomes less noticeable because of the tightening effect. The mask is rinsed off 10 to 15 minutes after application and its effects last for 8 to 10 hours. This is one of the only cases in which I recommend a product of my own along with only one other, simply because they are the only two effective products of this type that I know of.

TEMPORARY LIFTING MASKS

Nature Doctor's Aloe Lift Mask	M*
Zia Cosmetics Rejuvenating Lift Mask	M**

* Dr. Lois Blackhill, M.D., Miracle Manor, 12589 Reposo Way, Desert Hot Springs, CA 92240
**Zia Cosmetics, 1-800-334-SKIN

Another effective preventive treatment that helps to inhibit the aging of the neck is related to the way you sleep. If you sleep in a position that causes your neck to scrunch, it will create lines. Although these lines will disappear by midday, as you get older, they will become more persistent, until they are permanently etched into your skin. The way to avoid this is to learn to sleep on your back with your neck comfortably stretched out. It helps to purchase a neck pillow from any major department store or sleep shop. If you have never done it before, it will take time to adjust to this way of sleeping. But even if you only sleep part of the night in this position, it will help to save your neck. This is also the best way to sleep to minimize the formation of lines on the face.

Nonsurgical Salon Treatments

As with breast treatments, the only salon treatments I recommend for the neck and chin area are those that employ electrodermal stimulation. Most of these employ one of two machines: either the PDG (Paul Donat Groux) machine or the H.P. (Helen Pappas) machine. The procedures, called "non-surgical face lift" and "isotonic face lifting" respectively, are both offered in figure and facial salons.

Salon mask treatments applied to the neck are usually included as part of a facial, but are rarely as effective as the at-home lifting masks described earlier.

Acupuncture Lift

Another effective nonsurgical lift may be accomplished by acupuncture. The treatment is similar to the one described earlier for breast lift and augmentation. However, results will be seen sooner, sometimes immediately. A significant improvement will be noticed after three or four treatments. One patient who has undergone a series of treatments of the neck, chin, and face by Dr. Andy Soo Hoo, of San Francisco, states that after 15 treatments "people whom I have known for years are coming into my office and asking for me, not recognizing me or else calling me by my daughter's name. Before acupuncture, my cheeks were saggy, as were my eyelids, chin, and neck. Now they are firm and my skin looks and feels great." This patient also states that her body skin has improved and become less dry, her hair appears stronger and thicker, and she is experiencing "the most wonderful feeling of well-being that I have ever had." Dr. Soo Hoo explains that the additional benefits result from the overall toning of the entire body and internal organs caused by acupuncture treatments.

Maintenance treatments for acupuncture lift should be done every 1 to 3 months, depending on the patient.

Surgical Options

If your skin has degenerated too much to make any of the nonsurgical operations practical, you may want to consider surgery. Depending on your condition, there are three alternatives: the traditional chin tuck, the face lift, and the liposuction chin tuck.

CHIN TUCK (SUBMENTAL LIPECTOMY)

This operation is designed to correct a double chin, or "turkey wattle." An incision from 1 to 1 ½ inches long is made along the jawline under the chin in order to remove fatty deposits, fat cells, and excess skin. Then the skin is stitched up and the remaining scar, although visible, will not be seen unless the chin is lifted to expose it. Very few surgeons still use this method because a liposuction chin tuck is much simpler. On page 101, before and after photos show the results of a traditional chin tuck.

THE CLASSIC FACE LIFT

To perform the classic face lift (rhytidectomy), incisions are made in front of and behind the ears. Excess skin is then removed and the remaining skin is "draped" to have a natural look, then stitched at the incisions. If done correctly, the incision behind the ear will be hidden in the hair. The hairline, though almost always altered, should not have an unnatural appearance. The forward incision will be partially hidden in the lower portion of the ear and should not be obvious. When a face that has been lifted appears too tight, it is because the skin has been improperly draped. If you look in the mirror and place your middle finger above your jaw line and your index finger below, then pull back toward the ear, you will create the effect of a classic face lift.

Because this operation does not alter the upper portion of the face in any way, some cosmetic surgeons now believe that performing this lower lift by itself (without altering the upper portion of the face), creates an unnatural look. San Francisco cosmetic surgeon Dr. Robert Brink says that in the past few years "increasing emphasis has been given to treating the entire face as a unit rather than separating the forehead from the lower face merely because the patient has less concerns about the appearance of the forehead per se."

In Dr. Brink's experience, the lower face lift done without the upper face has a tendency to look "artificial or slightly peculiar." The addition of the upper face lift (brow or coronal lift) has many advantages—the adjustment of the anterior hairline either higher or lower, as a high hairline is unconsciously associated with advancing age, elimination of horizontal forehead folds and frown lines, and elevation of the eyebrow to its proper anatomical position on the brow bone, as this creates a more youthful, open eye.

To demonstrate his belief that a lower face lift by itself is not satisfactory, Dr. Brink uses before and after photos of one of his patients on whom he performed both a total (lower and upper) face lift. After photographing the results of his surgery, Dr. Brink cut the forehead portion of the before photograph and pasted it onto the after portion of the patient's lower face. Photo #1 was taken before surgery. Photo #2 is a composite of the patients forehead before surgery and her lower face after surgery. Photo #3 is the patient's face as it looks after the total face lift.

Photo #1, Before upper and lower face lift, (Dr. Robert Brink)   Photo #2, Composite photograph— Forehead, before lift, Lower face, after lift (Dr. Robert Brink)   Photo #3, After, total face lift (Dr. Robert Brink)

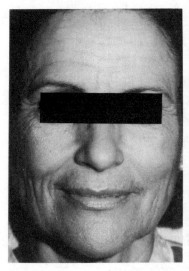 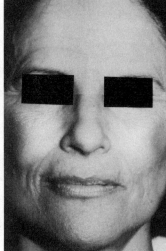 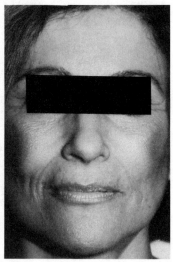

To see what effect coronal (upper face) surgery would have on you, look in the mirror and place the finger tips of both hands on your forehead, at the hairline. Gently lift the skin up with the finger tips until the hairy brows are directly over the brow bones. Now look at your eyes to see the effect that this has on your lids.

LIPOSUCTION CHIN TUCK

The liposuction chin tuck involves making a tiny incision, only ⅜ inch long, and sucking out the excess fat. However, if excess skin is also present, a larger incision will be needed to facilitate its removal. This is a simple operation that is usually done in an office surgical facility under local anesthesia and mild sedation. It takes between 1 and 2 hours and has a recovery time of 3 to 7 days. Although fat cells will not return, age and gravity may eventually cause the skin to sag. This varies greatly among patients, depending on their age, life-style, and skin condition.

The following before and after photos show the results of liposuction chin tuck as performed by Dr. Alan Gaynor.

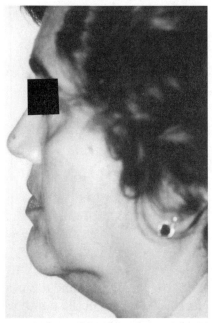

Patient before traditional chin tuck and face lift
(Dr. Robert Brink)

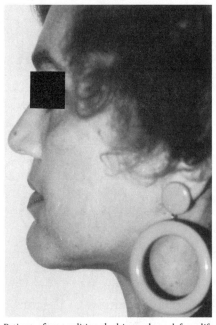

Patient after traditional chin tuck and face lift
(Dr. Robert Brink)

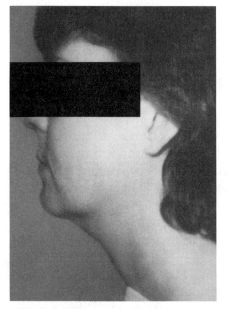

Patient before liposuction chin tuck and face lift
(Dr. Alan Gaynor)

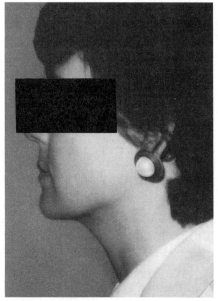

Patient after liposuction chin tuck and face lift
(Dr. Alan Gaynor)

C H A P T E R
NINE

HANDS, ARMS, AND FEET

It doesn't take a lot of time to maintain healthy, attractive hands, arms, and feet, just a little special know-how. You can make a great deal of difference in the appearance of these extremities by incorporating a few simple practices into your everyday cleansing routines.

At-Home Treatments for the Hands and Arms

DAILY TREATMENTS

You may remember the old dishwashing detergent commercials on television that showed two attractive women cavorting in the great outdoors, then challenged you to tell which one was 35 and which one was 19. I always tried to tell by looking at their faces, rather than their hands, but thanks to the magic of television, I was almost never right. These days, it is becoming increasingly more difficult to judge a woman's age by her face, but I can almost always tell by her hands. It's a shame that so many women who go to the trouble and expense of having a face-lift are betrayed by their hands. This need not be the case.

The two worst enemies of the hands and arms are ultraviolet light from the sun and housework. It's easy to protect yourself from these by wearing a total sun block on a daily basis and gloves when doing housework. Choose an oil-based block from Chapter 3 and use it like a hand lotion before leaving your house. Make sure to apply this to any exposed areas on your arms too. The oil and emollients will help to soften and moisturize your skin. Keep an extra tube in the glove compartment of your car, in case you've forgotten to apply it beforehand. This is also good in case you get caught in traffic on a sunny day and need to protect more than your hands. Then invest a dollar or two in a pair of cotton-lined rubber gloves and wear them faithfully whenever you wash dishes, rinse stockings, or do cleaning of any kind. Detergents, bleach, and cleansers are all very drying to the skin. Rubber gloves also help to protect nail polish and may add as much as 10 days to the life of a manicure.

Harsh winter weather can also be hard on your hands. Wearing warm gloves will protect you from the cold and wind, and help your hands to maintain their moisture balance. Going without gloves can cause hands to chap and even crack. To help heal hands with problems such as these, apply a coat of Aqualin Concentrate and cover with cotton gloves at night, then use a hand cream during the day.

Once you have mastered the two simple rules of wearing a sun block and protective gloves, there are several small, daily habits that, if practiced regularly, will also help you keep your hands looking young.

1. Gently push cuticles back with a towel after bathing.
2. Always apply a hand cream to damp hands and arms after washing—be sure to massage it into your cuticles.
3. Apply a rich cream or oil, such as vitamin E, or almond oil, to cuticles and hands at night. For extremely dry hands, apply a thin layer of Aqualin Concentrate and wear a pair of cotton gloves to sleep.
4. Carry a small tube of hand cream or Aqualin Light in your purse and use it often during the day.

One of the most common complaints that people have about their arms is caused by too much washing. It is a type of dry skin called keratosis pilaris and appears as tiny, hard bumps, usually on the outsides of the upper arms (or on the upper thighs). If you have this condition, remember that it is essentially dry skin, and treat it in the following way:

1. Take shorter baths and showers, and reduce the water temperature to comfortably hot, rather than very hot.
2. Do not use soap on the affected area unless it is actually dirty.
3. Use a loofah sponge or mitt in a gentle circular motion on the area every time you bathe.
4. After bathing, apply a moisturizer or body lotion to the area.

Elbows can become red, rough, and dry if not treated properly. When showering, use a loofah to gently remove dead, dry skin. Always apply a body oil or lotion after bathing and a rich moisturizer or oil such as Aqualin, or Zia Cosmetics Extra Emollient Hand & Foot Creme before going to bed.

SPECIAL TREATMENTS

Exfoliation   Here is an excellent beauty treatment for the hands, using an enzyme exfoliant (peel), that takes only 15 minutes and may be done as often as twice a week. An enzyme exfoliant contains different types of fruit or vegetable enzymes in a cream base. The most commonly used enzymes are papain and bromelain, from papaya and pineapple, respectively. The enzymes dissolve dead skin cells very effectively without the abrasiveness of a grainy cleanser and without harming young, new cells.

RECOMMENDED ENZYME EXFOLIANTS (PEELS)

Reviva Labs Light Skin Peel	H
Skinzyme	H
Zia Cosmetics Fresh Papaya Peel	H,M*

*Zia Cosmetics (1-800-334-SKIN), P.O. Box 143, Mill Valley, CA 94941.

Cleanse your hands and pat them dry. Apply an enzyme peel. Follow label directions regarding the length of time to leave the peel on. Remove as directed. Splash your hands generously with an aloe vera toner such as Nature's Way Aloe Vera Spray, available in health food stores, or Zia Cosmetics Sea Tonic With Aloe Toner. Let this dry completely, then apply a moisturizing mask such as Zia Cosmetics Super Hydrating Mask, or make one yourself by following the recipe below. Leave it on for 10 minutes, then rinse the mask off thoroughly with warm water. Pat your hands dry, and reapply the aloe vera product. While the hands are still damp with aloe, apply Zia Cosmetics Extra Emollient Hand & Foot Creme or any rich moisturizer and massage it well into your skin, remembering to gently push back your cuticles as you do so.

MOISTURIZING MASK

Mix together the following ingredients in a small bowl:

1 tablespoon plain yogurt   *1 egg yolk*
½ teaspoon honey   *1 vitamin E capsule*

Waxing   This is a simple beauty treatment for the hands that removes surface hairs and the outer layer of dead, dry cells. It is these cells that give the hands a parched, leathery look. When they are removed, fine lines will also disappear. The effects last for several days, and the procedure may be repeated as often as every 2 weeks. If you choose the waxing method, use it instead of the exfoliation method described above. You can alternate between the two by doing each one every other week.

In order to wax your hands, you will need either hot or cold wax. Choose one of the brands mentioned in Chapter 3. Prepare your hands by washing and drying them well. Then apply a light dusting of talcum powder, gently brushing off the excess with your fingertips. Apply the wax evenly across the back of your hand, *following the natural direction of hair growth,* between your wrist and your knuckles. Smooth a cloth strip over the wax and gently rub it in the same direction as application. Pull the cloth strip off in the opposite direction of application and immediately apply an antiseptic such as Sea Breeze with a cotton ball or pad. If you have sensitive skin, apply a thin paste made of baking soda mixed with water, and allow this to dry and remain on your hands. Once it has dried, you may brush off the excess soda with your fingertips. If your skin is not sensitive, apply an oil-based moisturizer instead of the baking soda mixture. Now compare the difference between that hand and the untreated one. Any redness will disappear in a few minutes, and your hand may have a tingly sensation for a few hours. Surface hair that has been removed by the wax will grow back in 4 or 5 weeks, but with repeated waxing will eventually grow back less and less. These hairs will not be stubbly when they regrow because they have been removed by the root and must grow in completely.

Manicures Nothing takes the place of a good, professional manicure, although at-home manicures help to maintain healthy nails and cuticles and give your hands a finished, polished look. Whether you are a professional, working woman or a homemaker, well-manicured hands are a must. Chipped nail polish and uneven, broken nails speak volumes about a woman.

To give yourself a manicure, allow approximately 20 minutes. First assemble the following items:

nail polish remover (nonacetone)

several cotton balls or pads

small bowl of warm water with a squirt of dishwashing detergent in it

soft, clean terry cloth towel

emery board

creamy or liquid cuticle remover

orange stick

nail brush

cuticle nipper

hand cream

base coat (non-formaldehyde)

nail polish (colored or clear) (non-formaldehyde)

top coat (non-formaldehyde)

Step 1. Remove all traces of old polish with a nonacetone polish remover and cotton balls.

Step 2. Wash your hands well with soap and water to remove all traces of polish remover. Dry hands well.

Step 3. Using the rough side of the emery board, file your nails straight across until they are the length you desire.

Step 4. Using the fine side of the emery board, shape your nails by filing them from the corner straight out toward the end of your nail. Keep the sides straight, rather than shaping them in, for more strength. If you prefer a rounded look, gently round the tips with the fine side of the board.

Step 5. Soak one hand in the sudsy water for 5 minutes.

Step 6. Apply cuticle remover to the hand that has been soaking. Wait 2 minutes.

Step 7. Using the rounded end of the orange stick, gently push back the cuticles. Try to keep the stick as parallel to the nail as possible.

Step 8. Using the nail brush, gently wash off the cuticle remover under warm, running water.

Step 9. Dry your hand and nails with the terry cloth towel and gently push back your cuticles as you do so.

Step 10. Use the cuticle nipper to cut away any hangnails, but do not attempt to cut your cuticles.

Step 11. Using the pointed end of the orange stick, gently clean under each nail.

Step 12. Repeat Steps 5 through 11 on the other hand.

Step 13. Apply hand cream and massage it well into hands and cuticles. Use the terry cloth towel to thoroughly wipe the hand cream off of your nails.

Step 14. Apply a base coat or ridge filler to all nails.

Step 15. Apply nail polish. Wait 5 minutes and apply another coat.

Step 16. Wait 5 minutes, then apply top coat.

Be sure to wait at least 10 minutes before using your hands, and even then, do so very carefully. It takes about 30 minutes for three coats of nail polish to dry completely. If you're in a hurry, immersing your nails in a bowl of ice water for 5 minutes will help the polish to set more rapidly.

One of the secrets of making a manicure last is to apply a top coat every other day. To really stretch it, you may also add a coat of color after a few days, then continue to add top coat over that. It is also important to get into the habit of not using your nails for daily chores such as opening soda cans, cleaning your teeth, turning small screws, and dialing phones. The less you use your nails, the stronger and prettier they will be.

Salon Treatments
For the Hands and Arms

MANICURES

The difference between a professional manicure and one you give yourself depends on how good you are and how good the manicurist is. A well-trained manicurist, and they are hard to find, will get rid of every trace of dead cuticle without causing you any pain, redness, or hangnails, will shape your nails perfectly, and will apply a quality of polish that will not chip for 2 weeks. She will also give a great hand massage. Very few women can equal this type of treatment on themselves, and as prices of beauty treatments go, manicures are still a bargain, ranging between $6 and $18, with $10 as the most common price.

Another advantage of a salon treatment is the option of a hot oil manicure. Instead of soaking your fingertips in the usual mixture of "soapy" water, hot oil or emollient cream is used. This type of manicure is great for someone with heavy or very dry cuticles, as it softens them completely, enabling the manicurist to effectively remove them. If you wish this type of manicure, be sure to specify so when making your appointment.

PARAFFIN

Some salons, often those that offer facials, are now offering paraffin treatments for the hands. This is just like having a facial on your hands. If given in conjunction with a manicure, it will be done before the polish is applied. Your hands are placed on a sheet of plastic wrap and massaged with an emollient cream or lotion. Hot, melted paraffin is then brushed on (this is comfortably hot and does not burn). The hands are then wrapped in plastic wrap and covered with towels to retain the heat of the wax. When the hands are unwrapped 15 minutes later, the paraffin is easily peeled away and the hands feel incredibly soft and smooth. This treatment is often done with a facial and is also performed on the feet.

At-Home Treatments
for the Feet

DAILY TREATMENTS

For our protection, the skin on the soles of the feet is the thickest skin on the entire body, approximately ten times thicker than other skin. Because of this, dead skin cells build up quickly, creating a tough outer layer that becomes concentrated on the heels and balls of the feet. If left untreated, this skin can become so dry that it eventually cracks.

Two simple, daily steps will help keep your feet soft and smooth. First, use a pumice stone or pumice-coated tool to slough away dead skin cells in the shower. Pumice is a natural, volcanic substance with a gritty texture and is commonly sold in pharmacies. Concentrate on heels, soles, little toes, and any area of your foot that tends to become callused. Dr. Scholl's and other manufacturers make several pumice tools that are readily available in pharmacies. They all work well provided they are used daily and only on wet feet. The hot water in a bath or shower softens the dead skin, making it easy to slough away. However, I do not recommend using a pumice on corns, as it will only cause irritation.

Once the dead skin cells on your feet have been removed, you can moisturize the new, softer skin to help discourage new calluses from forming. It is best to do this before going to bed. If you apply a moisturizer during the day, especially before putting on nylons, it will cause your feet to swell in your shoes. During the day, apply a cornstarch-based powder or foot powder to help absorb moisture before putting on stockings. If you are going stockingless in shoes, sprinkle powder into your shoes to help keep your feet dry. Always dry your feet well after bathing, making sure to dry between your toes and push back your cuticles.

To help keep the skin on your feet soft, I suggest massaging a therapeutic oil or lotion, with healing qualities, into your feet each night. This is also very relaxing, especially if you've been on your feet all day. You may even enroll your roommate or partner into doing this for you by offering to exchange rubs. Dr. Scholl's Foot and Leg Conditioning Lotion is especially for this purpose, and Dr. Hauschka's makes an invigorating herbal oil, Sage Foot Bath, which is available in health food stores, or you may just use aqualin concentrator or any rich, thick moisturizer.

SPECIAL TREATMENTS

For most of us, our feet spend the major portion of the day squeezed into shoes (which rarely resemble the natural shape of feet) and, as a result, often develop problems such as calluses and corns. Many people do not realize that foot problems even as small as these can affect their entire body. With proper care, these and other maladies of the foot can be greatly minimized and even prevented.

Callus is the buildup of skin that usually appears on the heel or ball of the foot. It is basically caused by the way you walk and for this reason is difficult to prevent. However, you can reduce the friction that causes calluses by inserting insoles into your shoes. Cushioned insoles, particularly the water-filled ones, can do wonders to alleviate this problem. They also provide a cushioning effect, which makes being on your feet less tiring. My favorite product of this type is called Aquasole. Aquasoles are filled with a solidified gel and are as "cushiony" as the water-filled insoles, but last longer. They can also be trimmed to size with ordinary scissors, and there is no danger of leakage. In addition, they are treated with a deodorant to help kill bacteria and keep both feet and shoes fresh. Aquasole may be found in some health food stores but can also be ordered by mail, toll-free, at 1-800-626-7888.

If you have a chronic callus, you should visit a podiatrist as it may be the result of a structural problem in your foot. If this is the case, surgery may be required.

Corns usually appear on the sole of the foot or on top of a toe. They are round and hard with a hard core at the center. They are the most easily prevented foot problem as they are almost always caused by ill-fitting shoes. Properly fitted shoes neither rub nor press against any part of your foot. Unfortunately, most fashionable shoes are designed to fit snugly, and as a result both rub and press. The only type of commonly worn shoe that measures up to a podiatrist's standards of good fit are aerobic or tennis style shoes. You can also do your feet a service by switching back and forth between these and heels. Wearing sneakers for walking to and from work—which has been the rage for several years—is actually very sensible.

Most podiatrists warn people to stay away from any type of home treatment for corns, including over-the-counter medications that contain an acid that can damage healthy tissue surrounding a corn. For proper removal of a corn, visit a podiatrist.

Blisters are caused by improperly fitted shoes rubbing against the skin. Soaking the foot in a pan of hot water containing ½ cup of Epsom salts will help to soothe a painful blister. You may then want to apply an antiseptic cream such as Neosporin (available over the counter at drug stores) and cover the blister with a soft gauze bandage. It is not good to pop blisters, as this can lead to infection. Obviously, the best way to avoid blisters is to wear comfortable, properly fitted shoes.

Ingrown toenails occur when a nail grows back into the skin. This is usually caused by toenails that are too long. In this case, the problem can be avoided by keeping your nails well trimmed. Sometimes chronic ingrown toenails are caused by a misshapen toe or toenail. If this is so, you may want to consult a podiatrist regarding correction of the problem.

Fungal infections such as athlete's foot require treatment that will kill the fungus that causes the infection. A doctor can prescribe a medicated ointment for this, or you may want to try a "natural" remedy. The most effective natural treatment that I know of calls for a daily application of tea tree oil. This is an extract taken from the Australian tea tree, imported by the Desert Essence company and available in health food stores.

The best way to prevent fungal infections is to keep your feet dry and free of perspiration. Remember to dry your feet well, apply a cornstarch-based or medicated foot powder, and remove socks and shoes after exercising. Allowing the feet to remain in damp, sweat-soaked socks and sneakers is an invitation to fungal and bacterial infections.

Foot odor If you are bothered by foot odor, there is a revolutionary product on the market called Lavilin Long Life Deodorant. (There are two products—one for the underarms and a stronger version for the feet.) Its unique, natural formula kills bacteria more effectively than any of the chemical foot deodorants on the market and it need only be used once every 7 to 10 days. Lavilin is available in health food stores and by mail order (call 1-800-LAVILIN).

Pedicures One of the best ways to keep your feet in good shape is to give yourself a pedicure. The procedure is almost exactly the same as a manicure, the only difference being that you soak your whole foot in warm water that contains a softening solution. You will also need to separate your toes from each other before applying polish. This may be done by rolling up a 12-inch length of bathroom tissue and weaving it between your toes. If you wish, you may prefer to purchase a set of foam rubber toe separators designed specifically for this use at a local beauty supply store. They cost about $1. Then follow the same steps as you would for a manicure.

A professional pedicure is a favorite luxury of many women. A good pedicurist can safely remove layers of callus by using a special tool; she can cut away all traces of dead cuticle, and give a very relaxing foot massage. This is a great way to get your feet ready for summer.

CHAPTER
TEN

SPECIFIC TREATMENTS

Pigmentation Correction

The most common pigmentation complaint that women have usually concerns "age spots"or "liver spots"—although they are not actually caused by age and doctors dispute the belief that they are related to the liver. These dark brown spots, medically referred to as *senile lentigines,* occur most commonly on the hands of women past the age of 30. They may also appear on the chest and face. The truth is that no one really knows what causes these spots. Many dermatologists believe them to be a result of hormones interacting with the sun. However, it is generally agreed upon that daily use of a total sun block will help prevent these spots from forming.

There are several types of topical treatment for age spots. You should discuss all of the treatments mentioned below with your doctor.

Electrocautery uses a fine platinum needle with an electric current running through it to burn off the spot. Little, if any, pain is involved, and the area heals completely within 7 days. This can be a safe, effective treatment for small lentigines.

Bleach creams are products containing 4 percent hydroquinone, a white, crystalline form of carbolic acid. These are sometimes effective when used over a period of time (6 weeks to 3 months), but a total sun block must be used in conjunction with these creams, or the skin will form more pigment and the spots become worse. Although commercial bleach creams are sold over the counter, they are neither as strong nor as effective as ones prescribed by a doctor. Hydroquinone may cause allergic reactions of redness or burning in some people, and if you have an allergic reaction to this, or any other cosmetic, its use should be discontinued immediately. For those not allergic, this ingredient is generally considered to be safe, provided it is not ingested—in which case it may cause nausea or vomiting.

Cryosurgery is performed in a doctor's office and may be the safest treatment to date. Liquid nitrogen is applied directly to "freeze" the spots. Within 3 days, a small scab forms. In a few more days it falls off, and the spot comes with it. There is a minimum of discomfort during treatment, and complete healing takes place within 10 days. This treatment is not recommended for those with very dark complexions as it may cause a temporary loss of pigmentation that may last as long as several months.

NATURAL CURES FOR AGE SPOTS

Many nutritionists and herbalists believe that it is possible to treat age spots by several different natural methods. One of the newest is the topical application of squalane, a nutrient-rich oil derived from shark liver or olives. To try this, apply the squalene to the affected area twice daily. Results should be visible within 3 months.

Another treatment uses the topical application of aloe vera in conjunction with drinking it daily. To try this treatment, apply pure aloe vera juice or gel to the affected area twice daily and drink 2 ounces of aloe vera juice in a large glass of water twice daily.

A third treatment is recommended by herbalist Linda Rector, owner of the Crystal Star Herb Company in Sonora, CA. Linda's treatment is based on the belief that toxins in the liver cause the spots. She recommended a three-day liver cleansing program of drinking 4 glasses of lemon juice and water daily. Also drink 4 ounces of lemon juice mixed with 4 ounces of olive oil, once daily, sipped through a straw. Then lie on your right side to facilitate absorption. In addition, take 2 tablespoons each of lecithin and brewer's yeast and drink six glasses of water daily.

It's a good idea to accompany this program with raw vegetable juices, but only for 2 to 3 days. For one month do not eat: red meats, oxalic acid-forming foods, sugars, refined starches, dairy products, alcohol, or caffeine. Do drink as much apple, cherry, or cranberry juice as you wish. Take 10 umeboshi plum balls daily to alkalize your system.

Vitamins A and E are also believed to help fight age spots from the inside of the body by fighting the effects of photoaging, or sun damage, aiding the production of collagen, and helping the cell growth processes of the skin. These are the average recommended dosages included in Chapter 2. Remember to allow at least 3 months before expecting to see results.

Scar Removal or Reduction

Many types of scars may now be improved, or "revised," with various combinations of techniques. Although corrective surgery itself leaves a scar, it will be much less obvious than the original, and in some cases barely visible to the naked eye.

The success of a scar revision depends on the type and location of the scar. Concave, or depressed, scars can be raised surgically or filled in with silicone, collagen (this is not permanent), or excess fat taken from your own body. This latter treatment, called "fat recycling," was popularized by Dr. Julius Newman, of Philadelphia, but may not be permanent either.

Raised, or elevated, scars are often treated with dermabrasion. Wide scars may be surgically narrowed, then smoothed out with this process. Dr. Norman Orentreich, a New York–based dermatologist, has perfected a technique called microdermabrasion in which he uses a tiny electric needle to remove the edges of scars or wrinkles. A long scar can be surgically shortened by recutting it to break up the length and straightness of the line. Some scars may be relocated by surgically pulling the skin to a nearby area where it may be hidden, such as the hairline, under the chin, or in a naturally occurring fold (such as the ear, nose, or eye).

Recovery time from a scar reduction or removal will vary greatly depending on the severity of the scar and the type of procedure used.

Plastic and reconstructive surgeons usually have the most experience in scar reduction and removal, but many dermatologists and otolaryngologists (ear, nose, and throat doctors) also do this type of surgery. To find the surgeon who is right for you, you may want to consult each type of doctor and review before-and-after photos of their work.

Dermabrasion

Dermabrasion is a method of removing several outer layers of skin by using electric brushes with fine steel heads. The purpose of the treatment is to shock the skin into producing new collagen and new skin that is free of the wrinkles and scars of the old skin. Dermatologists use this method more than plastic surgeons because it can be effective in removing scars resulting from acne. When used on small areas of the body, it usually is done with local anesthesia. Recovery time varies from 8 to 12 days, and makeup may not be worn for 10 to 12 days following the operation. The effects last only 1 to 1 ½ years, but the procedure may be repeated as often as every 2 years.

A new dermabrasion technique now being used by San Francisco cosmetic dermatologist Dr. Alan Gaynor now makes it possible for persons with dark skin to be dermabraded. Until recently, only those with fair skin could use the procedure to remove acne scars and lines and wrinkles. The new technique works because of advances in the post surgical dressings. With the new dressings, there is no scabbing and full makeup may be applied to the skin in about five days. In five days, men look as though they've had a "bad sunburn," Dr. Gaynor says. When used on acne scars, the effects of this procedure are permanent. The new dressings also mean that people may go out in the sun after five to seven days, provided they wear a sunblock with an SPF of 30. The new procedure also means that a woman with lines on the upper lip may have the operation done in that area only, without the fear of having different color skin. Another technique called "peelabrasion" combines a dilute solution of 35% TCA (trichloracetic acid) with dermabrasion and is even more effective for the lip area. Dr. Gaynor states that this procedure will remove 60 to 70% of lines for 5 to 10 years.

Chemical Peels

Chemical peels (chemosurgery) are used to remove lines and wrinkles as well as certain types of superficial scars. The effects last for 1 to 3 years and the procedure may be repeated every 2 to 3 years. Most doctors agree that chemical peels are more effective than dermabrasion, though more painful. They also can be more dangerous because they destroy the pigment-bearing cells known as melanocytes. With these cells gone, the skin's pigmentation is permanently lightened. For this reason, chemical peels are not appropriate for dark-skinned women. Change in pigmentation also makes skin extremely sensitive to ultraviolet rays; if exposed, brown spots or uneven pigmentation may develop. Skin that has been chemically peeled will never tan like unpeeled skin. However, brown spots that were removed by the peel will eventually return. Following a peel a patient must avoid any exposure to the sun for 3 months. During and after that time a sun block with an SPF of 15 or more must always be used.

The three chemicals commonly used in peeling today are resorcinol, trichloroacetic acid, and the original phenol/croton oil combination. If, applied too heavily or left on too long, the chemical peel may have other side effects. Dr. George W. Commons, a plastic surgeon on the staff of the University of California Medical Center, and former chief of plastic surgery for the U.S. Army, recommends doing "several conservative peels rather than one strong one" and advises against the popular practice of taping the skin—applying tape to the skin after the peeling substance has been applied. Taping creates a deeper peel but gives the practitioner less control.

Although there is some controversy about this, peels also are performed in salons by aestheticians. In fact, it was in a salon that this procedure was born. The type of peel used in salons is milder than that used by doctors, and the results are less effective. But the 7 to 12 days of inconvenience and discomfort for the patient are almost identical.

Until recently, I was against chemical peels because I had continually come up against so much contradictory information when interviewing dermatologists and facialists. However, I have since changed my opinion, based on interviews with plastic/cosmetic surgeons and photographs of results. Chemical peels can be incredibly beneficial to women with badly lined, degenerated skin. However, I would recommend consulting with a plastic/cosmetic surgeon or dermatologist rather than an aesthetician, and I would not recommend this procedure for younger women who just want to get rid of a few superficial lines.

Spider Vein Removal

Only one procedure exists for the permanent treatment of the superficial (not raised) red veins that usually appear on the legs. This procedure uses a 24.4 percent sodium chloride solution injected directly into the veins. The solution, which is 24 times stronger than the one found naturally in human blood, causes the vein to shrink and dry up. The salt water actually kills the veins, which are considered "extra veins" and not needed for proper bodily function since they serve no medical purpose. Treatment is performed in a doctor's office, with or without the use of a local anesthetic. The veins disappear within 5 to 7 days.

Although some doctors use electrocautery (discussed on page 111) for the treatment of superficial veins, it is not recommended because it is temporary.

Varicose Vein Removal

The bulging, blue veins that occur on the legs are hereditary and a result of the pull of gravity. These veins are considered to be reservoirs and serve no medical function other than the storage of extra blood. As they become more enlarged, the valves that prevent blood from falling back into them become incompetent, and the veins become even more engorged.

The treatment used for the removal of varicose veins is known as stripping, and must be performed by a vascular surgeon. The operation involves making small incisions in the ankles and below the knees, into which a metal instrument is inserted and used to pull the veins out of the legs. The recovery may be painful and takes up to 2 weeks, although it may be as long as 6 weeks before a patient is able to exercise vigorously. The only resulting scars may be left by the small incisions. Stripping is not permanent. Although veins cannot replace themselves or regrow, others will become varicose later.

CHAPTER
ELEVEN

THE BEST OF AMERICAN SPAS

In writing this book, my intention was to find American spas that offer a full range of exercise, nutritional meals and counseling, and stress management along with European-style treatments for the body. European-style treatments are traditionally more advanced because of their long history of medically based research. Many European spas have been in existence for as long as three hundred years and offer medical as well as beauty treatments. For this reason, I chose to focus on the European-style spas. I was surprised to find that only four such spas exist in the United States, but I was not at all disappointed in the spas themselves. Two of these spas will be reviewed at the end of this chapter. The third spa, the Norwich Inn & Spa, was completely booked during the times I was available to visit, so I am unable to give you a firsthand report. The fourth spa preferred not to be included in a book. I also discovered several other types of spas that are well worth visiting. It appears that even a short stay at a good all-around spa can do more for your mind and body than most ordinary vacations.

What a Spa Can Do for You

Many people have discovered that a stay at a spa can alleviate the mental and physical symptoms of stress that so often accompany a demanding job or family life. Some people use spas to get started on a regular exercise program or to lose weight and learn better eating habits; still others go to spas for a spiritual retreat. I'm going to give you some general background information about different types of spas and what they offer because spa trips can no longer be categorized as mere "luxury vacations for the idle rich"—although some spas do specialize in giving their guests the opportunity to do nothing!

How to Choose the Right Spa

To help you decide which spa is right for you, you must first evaluate your goals. Also, be aware of the fact that as your needs change, what you want from a spa will also change. For example, after the winter holidays you may want to visit a spa to lose a few extra pounds and get into shape. By the summer, you may want to learn meditation, or just get away to relax for a few days. Before choosing a spa, first consider the following categories and decide what's important to you.

Antistress/relaxation

Weight loss/learning and establishing better nutritional habits

Body contouring/exercise

Personal growth/spiritual improvement

Vacation/sports

Postoperative recuperation

Beauty makeover

If you are interested in losing weight, you will want to visit a spa that not only offers tailor-made diets and exercise programs, but also provides you with information on how to continue eating and exercising properly when you leave. There's no point in visiting a spa and losing several pounds only to return home, resume old habits, and gain them all back. Learning about nutrition and exercise in the healthy atmosphere of a spa, where you are able to practice good habits as you learn them, has a much greater impact than reading a book or taking a class. Many spas also offer support material in the form of charts, diagrams, recipes, meal plans, and videos. These are designed to help you incorporate what you have learned at the spa into your life at home.

Jeffrey Joseph's *Spa-Finders* catalog is an excellent publication that lists and briefly describes approximately 140 American spas. Spas are categorized according to what they offer and their location. The magazine is done very nicely; however, no addresses or phone numbers are given. All information may be obtained through Jeffrey Joseph's travel agency. For information write *Spa-Finders,* 784 Broadway, New York, NY 10003-4856; or call 1-800-ALL-SPAS (in New York State, 1-212-475-1000).

Hot Mineral Springs Spas

One of my favorite types of spa is that built around natural hot mineral springs. Calistoga, California, which has an abundance of these springs, is famous for this type of spa. The waters contain high levels of various minerals and nutrients, and like other hot springs around the world, are often attributed curative powers for a variety of ills from arthritis to constipation. There is very little hard evidence available in this country to support such claims. But spagoers will dispute this vehemently, claiming to have been cured from hundreds of different ailments. Spas centered around these springs usually offer pools, tubs, Jacuzzis, and steams that are filled with this water. Many of the Calistoga spas also offer "mud baths" made from local volcanic ash mixed with the local mineral water. These are great for sore muscles and provide deep relaxation along with detoxification. However, none of the Calistoga spas are designed with luxury in mind. The accommodations resemble two-story motels and some rooms have kitchenettes. Many were built in the thirties and forties and remain much the same as they were originally. They can be charming, if you are fond of that time period and don't expect modern amenities such as thick carpeting, luxurious bathrooms, or modern furniture. These spas offer neither exercise programs, nor dining facilities, nor nutritional guidance. Most do offer hot tubs, pools, Jacuzzis, mud baths, steams, massage, and blanket wraps.

A typical hot springs treatment takes about 3 hours and leaves you feeling relaxed as a limp noodle. For example, if you visit the Calistoga Spa, a typical treatment would proceed as follows: You arrive at 10:00 A.M. and are assigned a locker in a newly renovated changing area. You are also given a large cotton flannel sheet to wrap around yourself after you've undressed. Once undressed, you are asked to shower and then proceed to the tub room. In this room are several large tubs filled with thick, black mud. You lie on top of the hot mud as an attendant scoops it over your body until you are completely covered, except for your face. The attendant places a cold cloth across your forehead to help keep you cool, while you lie perfectly still, covered with mud. Your body heats up rather quickly as the mud makes you sweat and begins to draw toxins out of your body. It also softens the outer layer of dead, dry cells, so that they may be removed at a later time. After 10 minutes in the mud, you slide out and shower off. While you are still wet, you are placed in a private Jacuzzi tub filled with hot mineral water. You lie back with your head resting on an inflatable pillow, and the cold cloth is once again placed on your forehead. The Jacuzzi bubbles you for 20 minutes. Upon stepping out of the tub, you are handed a cold glass of Calistoga mineral water to drink, and as soon as you've caught your breath, you are placed in a steam room that is heated with natural, mineral steam. You can stay as long as you wish, although most people spend only 5 minutes in the steam. This is the time to gently use a washcloth to remove all of the softened, dead skin cells from your body. As you leave the steam room you are offered more mineral water to drink and are shown to your private cubicle for the blanket wrap.

In a small private room, you lie down on a bed and are first wrapped in cotton blankets, then covered with wool ones. This feels like a cocoon, and you may choose to have your arms inside or outside of the wrapping. The cold cloth is replaced on your forehead, and you lie still, while your heart pounds from the prolonged, intense heat, and you sweat through at least two sets of cotton blankets. This is a sign that your body is releasing excess water along with toxic waste. During the next 30 to 40 minutes, many people either fall asleep or enter a meditative state. When the blanket wrap is removed, you are ready for your massage. This may be one of several types of massage, such as the classic, Swedish, or Oriental Shiatsu, which you choose at the time you book your treatment. After the massage I'm usually able to drag my body to the nearest deck chair and pass out, but rarely able to string words together to form a sentence. This series of treatments is the most intensely relaxing I have ever had. It is also the least expensive—the full price is approximately $25.

The remainder of the day is spent in the kind of bliss we imagine that clams bask in. I highly recommend having dinner in a local restaurant, not only because excellent food abounds in this small town, but also so you don't break the relaxation spell by getting into a car and driving somewhere.

Three of the best Calistoga spas are:

The Calistoga Spa, 1006 Washington St., Calistoga, CA 94515, 707-942-6269

Golden Haven Hot Springs Spa and Motel, 1713 Lake St., Calistoga, CA 94515, 707-942-6793

Dr. Wilkerson's Spa, 1507 Lincoln Ave., Calistoga, CA 94515, 707-942-4102

The Mount View Hotel, having been restored to its original Art Deco opulence several years ago, is the only "luxury" hotel in Calistoga. It has an excellent dining room, mirrored Art Deco bar with nightly entertainment, and a private, quiet pool area. Although the hotel does not offer any spa treatments, there are about six spas (including the three mentioned above) within walking distance where you can go for the day.

Two hot springs spas that offer more than day treatments are the Esaln Institute in Big Sur, California, and Two Bunch Palms. The Esalen Institute is a rustic retreat that offers a continually changing variety of learning programs and seminars. If you enjoy being a participant in the human potential movement, Esalen is for you. Two Bunch Palms, in Desert Hot Springs, California, is a small, luxurious resort-type spa. It also offers some of the most stupendous scenery in the world. For a sumptuous, romantic getaway, Two Bunch Palms is the best choice.

All-Around Spas

If you envision an all-around spa that provides planned meals, a variety of exercise programs, treatments (massage, facials, etc.), and instruction in areas such as cardiovascular fitness and low-calorie meal planning, you will enjoy a classic spa such as The Oaks at Ojai, The Heartland Health and Fitness Retreat, or The Sonoma Mission Inn and Spa.

Three All-American Spas

THE OAKS AT OJAI
122 East Ojai Ave., Ojai, CA 93023,
805-646-5573

The Oaks at Ojai is located in the small artists' village of Ojai, California. Although it is in the town itself, the individual bungalows and wood-paneled main building with a fireplace give you the feeling of a rustic mountain lodge. It is quiet, despite the fact that it is not secluded.

The emphasis at The Oaks is on health and fitness. There are 18 different classes and activities offered every day, and you choose which to participate in. There is absolutely no feeling of regimentation. If you're an early riser, or want to see what it's like to be one, you can begin the day at 6:00 A.M. with an aerobics class, or at 6:30 with a 6- to 8-mile mountain hike.

If these activities seem too early or too strenuous, you may want to wait until 7:00 A.M. and join the 3-mile "brisk walk." If you would rather sleep in, wait until 7:30 for a slow-paced, 1 ½-mile nature walk. Those who wish to relax more than work out may prefer to begin their day with breakfast, rather than exercise. This meal is served between 7:45 and 9:15. Between 8:00 A.M. and noon, five different fitness classes—aerobics, yoga, weight training, pool exercise, and stretching—are offered, along with instructional lectures whose subjects change each day.

THE HEARTLAND HEALTH AND FITNESS RETREAT
18 East Chestnut Street, Chicago, IL 60611 (business office),
312-266-2050

The Heartland Health and Fitness Retreat is a California-style spa in Gillman, Illinois, the heart of the Midwest. The property, once a private estate, is beautiful, quiet, and restful. The spa program is designed for those people interested in beginning a program of physical fitness. Educational and physical fitness classes are geared toward stress management, weight control/nutrition, and exercise.

The Heartland has the feeling of a summer camp for adults. Upon arrival, guests are issued all of the clothing they will need, with the exception of swimming suits, leotards, and exercise shoes. Since the spa only hosts 28 guests at a time, people are really able to get to know one another and a feeling of camaraderie develops quickly.

Meals are served in a small dining room, with tables of eight to ten, and the cuisine is gourmet, low-calorie vegetarian. Upon request, fish is served at dinner, and bowls of fresh fruit are available to guests throughout the day.

The Heartland is an excellent spa for the person who is interested in developing a more health-conscious life-style. It is actually more of a learning center than most spas. However, I do not recommend it for the person who is already in good shape and seeking either very challenging or advanced physical instruction.

THE SONOMA MISSION INN AND SPA
18140 Sonoma Highway, Sonoma, CA 95476,
707-938-9000 or 1-800-862-4945

Northern California is the home of The Sonoma Mission Inn, one of the loveliest hotel/spa resorts that I know of. This sprawling, gracious complex, originally built around natural hot springs, was luxuriously refurbished several years ago. The elegant five-star dining room is one of the best anywhere. Guests can choose from either the regular or the spa menu. There is also a more casual, California diner–type restaurant that serves delicious food all day long.

The spa facility is separate from the hotel and connected by a footpath. It is luxuriously furnished and elegant, giving guests a feeling of being pampered. The spa also has its own swimming pool, which is quieter and less crowded than the hotel pool.

Spa activities are offered from 7:00 A.M. to 7:15 P.M., although the spa facilities remain open for guests' use until 10:00 P.M. The wide range of activities includes hiking, tennis, all levels of aerobics classes, stretch and tone classes, weight training, aquarobics, and yoga. Individual instruction is always available in the circuit training room for those unfamiliar with the sophisticated Keiser machines.

The Sonoma Mission Inn and Spa also offers a full range of body and beauty treatments including herbal wrap, facial, manicure, pedicure, hair and scalp treatment, massage, and hydromassage. Although it is not unusual for many spas to offer these treatments, in my experience they are usually inferior to ones available in most salons. At this spa, these treatments were of exceptionally high quality. In fact, the facial was one of the best I have ever had. For the seasoned spagoer, treatments of this quality, along with the luxurious rooms, delicious food, and excellent variety of exercise programs, make The Sonoma Mission Inn and Spa an exceptionally good choice.

Here is a partial list of some other favorite all-around, all-American spas:

Canyon Ranch Vacation/Fitness Resort, 8600 East Rockcliff Road, Tucson, AZ 85715, 602-749-9000

Loews Ventana Canyon Resort, 7000 North Resort Drive, Tucson, AZ 85715, 602-299-2020

The Greenhouse, Box 1144, Arlington, TX 76010, 817-640-4000

Safety Harbor Spa and Fitness Center, 105 N. Bayshore Drive, Safety Harbor, FL 34695, 1-800-237-0155

Russell House of Key West, 611 Truman Avenue, Key West, FL 33040, 305-294-8787

The Golden Door, P.O. Box 1567, Escondido, CA 92025, 619-744-5777

Innovative
European-Style Spas

GURNEY'S INN

To get to Gurney's you can either drive or take a train from Manhattan to easternmost Long Island, which is approximately a 3 ½-hour trip, or take a small plane from New York's LaGuardia Airport to East Hampton. Long Island Air and East Hampton Air both fly this route. The planes to East Hampton carry a maximum of ten passengers; however, I was the only one on my flight, which added a certain feeling of luxury to the trip. A van will pick you up at the tiny airport at East Hampton, and drive you the remaining 30 minutes of the trip to Montauk Point, the very tip of Long Island.

Gurney's Inn and Spa, Montauk, New York

My first impression upon entering the lobby of Gurney's Inn was how large and bustling it was, for I had forgotten that it is a hotel as well as a spa.

One of Gurney's best features is the fact that it is situated on the ocean. All rooms, including both dining rooms, face a long stretch of white beach. Even though it was early spring when I visited, and quite cold at night, I kept the deck door to my room ajar while I slept so that I could hear the waves. Gurney's takes advantage of the therapeutic value of the sea in every way possible, using filtered sea water in their pools, Jacuzzis, and baths, and offering outside treatments, when the weather permits. It is the only spa in America to do this, and it made a real difference in my enjoyment of the facilities and treatments.

The attitude at Gurney's is unpretentious, comfortable, and efficient. There is no regimentation here, and each guest chooses a schedule of treatments and classes that suits his or her personal needs.

On my first day I was told that I had a choice of eating in the "regular" dining room, or the "spa" dining room. I chose the regular dining room, where the menu offered a large selection of fresh fish, veal, chicken, salads, and pastas. Everything I ate for the duration of my 3-day stay was perfectly prepared and delicious. I found the spa menu to be delicious as well. People who are not concerned with weight loss will appreciate having a full menu to choose from, while those desiring a limited caloric intake can enjoy truly gourmet, low-calorie, low-fat meals.

After a long walk on the beach I began to feel the healing benefits of the fresh sea air. Some believe that negatively charged ions are responsible for this, while others point out the possibility that all life began in the sea. It is also interesting to note that seawater is almost identical to human plasma. Whatever the explanation, the sense of well-being when near the sea is almost universally acknowledged.

At 4:20 I took a yoga class and realized how "stressed out" my body really was. By the end of the class I vowed to take as many as I could during my stay.

Following the class I had a seaweed wrap. This treatment is becoming quite popular in this country. The seaweed for Gurney's wrap is produced in Saint-Malo, France, by Goemar Labs, the foremost processor of seaweed in the world. It is a "seaweed cream," which looks much like a thick, pale green lotion and contains living cell extracts of fresh seaweed, derived by a patented process called "micronization." Due to its small cell structure, the seaweed is able to penetrate the skin very efficiently; its nutrients help the skin release toxins and nourish itself. However, one of the most noticeable effects of this treatment is the way your skin looks and feels afterward. It is incredibly soft, smooth, and moist. The seaweed is also an exceptionally effective exfoliant.

At Gurney's, the attendant applies the warm seaweed cream with her hands, using sweeping movements much like a Swedish massage. After it has been applied to your entire body (except the face), you are covered with a thin, waterproof sheet. Hot, wet towels are then placed over this to help keep in the heat and, finally, a blanket is used to cover all of the layers. The lights are then dimmed and the already-soft music is lowered. I rested in this peaceful state for 20 minutes while the seaweed did its work. The wraps were then removed and the attendant sponged the excess seaweed from my body. I was then taken to a "Swiss Shower," which is like a large stall shower with jets covering all of the walls and ceiling. The spray from the jets is very sharp, which is why it is sometimes referred to as a needle spray. The attendant adjusted the temperature of the water, alternating from hot to cool, for about 2 minutes. After the shower, I dried off and was wrapped in a thick, terry cloth robe. The attendant told me to rest for 20 minutes before getting dressed, and to not use soap on my body for several hours. I noticed that my skin felt incredibly smooth and soft, and I felt very relaxed.

I began the next day with another walk on the beach, and then was given my first hot "fango" treatment. Applied hot or cold, fango is a deep-penetrating mud treatment. It took place in a small, quiet, dimly lit room. The fango was placed on my upper back, shoulders, and neck, and I was surprised at the amount of perspiration it caused in that area. I do not sweat easily, even during strenuous exercise, so I could tell how extraordinarily effective this treatment was. Afterward, I felt very relaxed and sat quietly for about 20 minutes to regain my strength. I was glad that all I had to do next was eat lunch.

After lunch I had a "brush and tone" treatment, which is the same as dry brushing. It is designed to increase circulation on the entire body (except the face), and exfoliate dead skin cells. It consisted of a full body brushing with a brush stiff enough to scrub floors with. The attendant began brushing at my feet, using sweeping movements toward my heart. Although my skin did feel incredibly alive after this treatment, it was very painful. This is the only spa treatment I have ever had in which I wanted to scream "Stop!" Baroness Von Mengersen explained that this particular type of brush, made from synthetic fibers, is used at Gurney's because it can be sterilized. I have since discovered that boar bristle brushes work just as well without hurting. But this type of natural bristle brush doesn't hold up to the heat or chemicals necessary for sterilization. I was also told that the alternative to this treatment is a "salt glow" or "salt rub," in which coarse salt is massaged all over the skin to garner the same results. The Baroness assured me that this was even rougher. I would skip this treatment at a spa unless a boar bristle brush or loofah mitt is used.

During my next yoga class, which followed the body brushing, I noticed how much more relaxed I was than the day before. I felt more limber, my muscles were more willing to stretch, and my jaw wasn't constantly clenched. By this time, not a dead cell was left on my entire body, and I was glad that all I had on the schedule was an early dinner.

The next morning, after my ritual beach walk, I experienced thalasso-therapy, Gurney's style. The difference between this treatment and the hydro massage described in Chapter 4 is that Gurney's uses seawater. Of all the spas I visited, this treatment was the best, by far, at Gurney's. Although it took only 30 minutes, I felt as if I'd had a massage of an hour or more. It was incredibly relaxing and worked every ounce of tension and soreness from my body.

After my final treatment it was clear to me that the best had been saved for last. I am referring to an aromatherapy massage. This is not an ordinary type of massage, although you do lie naked on a table in a dimly lit room filled with quiet music. The purpose of this particular massage is to balance your mind as well as your body. Using mixtures of fragrant, herbal oils, the masseur, an exceptionally gentle, soft-spoken gentleman named Paul Kunkle, was able to relax my body and mind totally in about 30 seconds. He also imparted an extraordinarily strong sense of well-being that made me forget about all my problems and work, and elicited a proposal of marriage from me! (The Baroness later told me that Paul gets about four proposals a day.) It is rare to find such a capable therapist, and I hated to see the session end.

The unique aspect of an aromatherapy massage is the therapist's ability to direct your emotions through your sense of smell. In the beginning of the massage, Paul used a combination of ylang-ylang, chamomile, frankin-cense, and sweet almond extracts to create a calming effect—almost in-stantly. During the massage he used a combination of mint, pine, and rosemary for a medicinal or healing effect. To help me "regain conscious-ness" at the end of the massage, he used a combination of lemon, gera-nium, and coriander. I was amazed at the way my body and mind responded by becoming instantly alert.

I highly recommend an aromatherapy massage. Whether you are fortunate enough to visit Gurney's and experience Paul Kunkle, or whether you simply visit a local practitioner, it's well worth it. It is not only relaxing, but it also helps to establish a deep sense of well-being.

After 3 days at Gurney's I felt as if I'd been away for at least 2 weeks. Although many people associate a beach resort with the summer season, I

Thalassotherapy treatment, Gurney's Inn and Spa, Montauk, New York

thoroughly enjoyed the crisp air of early spring. I think it would be beautiful and equally enjoyable in the winter. This is a very special place to heal the mind and body or just spoil yourself.

THE DORAL SATURNIA INTERNATIONAL SPA RESORT
8755 N.W. 36th Street, Miami, FL 33178,
305-593-6030

The Doral Saturnia International Spa Resort officially opened its doors on September 1, 1987. It is, quite simply, the most exquisite and luxurious spa I have ever visited.

Modeled after the 300-year-old Terme di Saturnia spa in Tuscany, Italy, the Doral combines the best of American fitness and nutrition with European relaxation and skin care techniques. It is approximately a 10-minute drive from the Miami airport and next door to the Doral Country Club. The facilities at the country club—five championship golf courses, pool, 15 tennis courts, and world-class equestrian center—are all available for spa guests' use, as well as the extensive spa facilities: large outdoor recreational pool with Jacuzzi and cascading waterfalls to stand under for hydro massage; outdoor lap pool; indoor exercise pool; indoor, climate-controlled, banked track; outdoor exercise trail featuring exercise stations; four fully equipped exercise studios with two spring-loaded floors for safe aerobics classes; aqua-robics; yoga; stretch and tone classes; circuit weight training; steam rooms; saunas; whirlpools; cold plunges; and private, separate men's and women's sun decks for nude sunbathing. The country club also offers two dining rooms and a discotheque, as well as several shops carrying everything from diamonds to golf shoes. The only thing this complex is lacking is an ocean front location. But Miami Beach is only a 20-minute drive away, and guests are welcome to use any of the facilities at the Doral-on-the-Ocean, in Miami Beach. In fact, a shuttle bus service operates every day between the two properties.

The spa was built at a cost of $30 million, and you can see how this money was spent everywhere you look. From the moment you approach this incredible complex you are transported to what appears to be a lush, tropical version of Italy. It is an architectural feast for the eyes with formal old-world gardens, clay-tiled rooftops, and a 100-foot atrium that houses the more casual of the spa's two spectacular restaurants. Every detail, down to the silverware, has been flawlessly planned by a team of experts.

The attentiveness shown by the staff is extraordinary and makes each guest feel comfortable and cared for. The designer clothing that is issued to

Courtyard, the Doral Saturnia International Spa Resort, Miami, Florida

each guest, each day, as they check in for their day at the spa, includes sweat pants, T-shirt, cardigan sweat shirt, running shorts, leotard, terry cloth bathrobe, and cushioned rubber sandals—all of wonderful color, design, and quality. These make it easy to relax between treatments or have lunch without having to put on one's street clothes.

I found the spa treatments to be of the highest quality. My first day began with a health screening and fitness assessment. During this time blood was drawn by a registered nurse to determine my blood count and cholesterol level. My blood pressure was also checked, and I filled out a health-history questionnaire. The fitness director then tested my flexibility, lung function, grip strength, and percentage of body fat, and made suggestions for improvement. This fitness examination was the most complete of any I've had at a spa.

My first taste of the spa was a light stretch class, followed by a weight-training session. The David Machines, similar to but more advanced than Nautilus equipment, are the smoothest I have ever tried. An hour after a delicious lunch of the freshest garden salad, broiled red snapper, risotto with porcini mushrooms, and a fresh fruit sorbet, I had a light, Swedish massage. This was followed by a hydrotherapy treatment that was almost identical to the one I'd had at Gurney's. The only differences were the style of tubs and the water. The Doral's water was reconstituted, rather than fresh seawater.

The walls, floors, and ceilings of the treatment rooms are of gray and beige marble, inlaid in geometric designs with soft, lighted orbs in the middle of the walls for light. Soft flute or piano music is piped throughout the entire complex, including the locker rooms, so that the relaxing continuity of the place is never disturbed.

The locker rooms contain everything a woman or man might need, including hair dryers, shampoo, conditioner, shaving gel, after shave, powder, moisturizers, body lotions, hair mousse, hair spray, and mouthwash.

On the following day the real spa treatments began with a massage by a woman who is a true massage therapist. She knew exactly which muscles of my body were holding tension and went to work releasing it. The massage was followed by a back fango, which was a totally different treatment than the one I'd had at Gurney's.

At the Doral, the fango treatment is more like a facial for the back. It begins with a cleansing of the entire back from neck to buttocks. An exfoliant cream is then applied and a soft electric brush is used to remove it, along with the dead skin cells. A vaporizing steam is then applied for 10 minutes to open the pores and draw out toxins. Any clogged pores, blemishes, or blackheads are then removed. Next, a cream is applied—the type depends on your skin type and condition. This is followed by the application of comfortably hot paraffin (wax), which helps the cream to penetrate and soften the skin. After about 10 minutes the paraffin is removed in one piece and a toning cream is applied. The paraffin is not used on guests with broken capillaries or oily or acne-prone skin. For the final step, the fango mud is applied, but this fango is a cool, creamy substance that contains menthol, which causes a tingling sensation. The fango is made from reconstituted plankton and mud, imported from Italy. It is left on for 15 minutes—it does not harden—and then removed with soft, natural sponges. Finally, the skin is cleaned with an herbal toner and a moisturizer is applied. My friend told me afterward that my skin "glowed."

Cool fango treatments are also used on other parts of the body to treat problems that are untreatable with heat, such as varicose veins, bloating from water retention, and circulation problems.

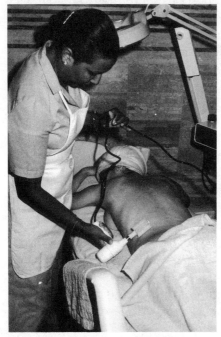

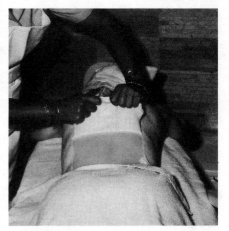

Exfoliation at the Doral Saturnia International Spa Resort

Paraffin removal during fango treatment at the Doral Saturnia International Spa Resort

On my last day at the Doral Saturnia I had a face fango that utilized the same paraffin and cold, mentholated fango I'd had for the back treatment. It was a very effective deep-cleansing, conditioning treatment, and the facialist, Regina Kipnes, was an absolute fountain of knowledge. Originally from Russia, Regina had been a licensed aesthetician there for many years. In Russia and many other Eastern European countries, aestheticians are required to take 4 years of premed training, which qualifies them to be pharmacists. This training is necessary because they make all of their own skin care preparations, many of which contain drugs. I could have spent days swapping recipes and knowledge with Regina, and I was sorry not to have the time. She was kind enough to give me some of her favorite product recipes, which I now pass on to you. These products are best if used immediately after you prepare them, unless otherwise indicated.

All recipes should be mixed in a glass or pottery bowl. The masks should be applied to clean skin on the entire face and neck area. Leave them on for 10 to 15 minutes, then rinse off with tepid water.

MASK FOR OILY SKIN

*1 tablespoon cottage or farmer
    cheese*
1 egg yolk
*1/4 cup grated cucumber (or
    mashed strawberries or
    blueberries)*

Pinch of fresh dill
Powdered milk

Mix together the first four ingredients and add the powdered milk a little at
a time to thicken.

MASK FOR ACNE AND/OR OILY SKIN

2 tablespoons brewers' yeast
2 tablespoons milk

1 egg white

Mix together all ingredients.

MASK FOR ALL SKIN TYPES*

1/2 papaya, crushed
1 egg yolk
1 tablespoon honey
1 capsule vitamin E or vitamin A

*1 ampoule collagen or elastin
    (optional; may be obtained
    from some facial salons)*

Mix together all ingredients.

* This mask may be stored for 2 to 3 days in the refrigerator.

DRY SKIN MASK #1

*2 tablespoons farina (Cream of
    Wheat)*

Milk

Mix enough milk with the farina to make a medium thick paste.

DRY SKIN MASK #2

1 tablespoon olive oil
1 teaspoon honey

1 egg yolk
Few drops fresh lemon juice

Mix together all ingredients.

DRY SKIN MASK #3*

Small pot of boiling water	*1 teaspoon olive oil*
1 whole lemon	*1 capsule vitamin E*
1 egg yolk	*1 capsule vitamin A*

Place lemon in the boiling water. Remove from heat, cover, and let stand for 10 minutes. Put the lemon into a food processor or blender with the remaining ingredients.

* This may be stored for 3 to 4 days in the refrigerator.

ALL-PURPOSE MOISTURIZER FOR DRY SKIN

Regina says there are many recipes for dry-skin preparations that include chocolate, possibly because of the rich oils and butter fat it contains, but also because chocolate acts as a preservative. This moisturizer will last up to a year if kept refrigerated. To help ensure its freshness, I also recommend using a clean spoon or spatula to take the cream out of the jar each time you use it. If you begin to notice any change in the way the product smells or looks, throw it away and make up a fresh batch.

1 egg yolk	*1 ampoule placenta (optional;*
1 tablespoon olive oil	*available in some facial salons)*
1 capsule vitamin E	*1 square melted chocolate (pure*
1 capsule vitamin A	*and imported is best)*

Mix all ingredients together and place in a sterilized, tightly covered glass jar. Store in the refrigerator.

My spa visit ended with another massage followed by an herbal wrap. The second massage removed every last trace of tension and stress from my muscles. However, I did not care for the herbal wrap. This particular method entailed lying on a table that had been covered with sheets previously soaked in boiling water and herbs. Despite the fact that a layer of towels was placed between them and my body, the sheets still felt too hot on my skin. Additional layers were placed over my body and a cold cloth was placed on my forehead. I prefer the previously described method of body wrap, which makes you sweat from the inside, rather than a direct application of heat to the skin.

The hotel accommodations at the Doral Saturnia International Spa Resort are nothing short of exquisite. There are only 48 rooms, and all are suites; 36 Luxe Suites have living rooms, entertainment centers (VCR, compact disc player, tape deck, stereo, television), and two European marble Jacuzzi baths with dressing rooms. Furnishings are of a sumptuous, modern Italian design and every room has a private patio and spectacular view of the lush grounds. The five Supreme Suites combine a Luxe Suite with an even more expansive Grand Suite, each designed on the theme of an Italian city.

The restaurants at the Doral feature some of the best food I have ever eaten, although it is all wholesome, low-fat, and low-calorie. The young chef, Michael McVay, began at a small restaurant in San Diego, California, which closed its doors after he left. He then served as head chef at the Golden Door for 3 years, followed by 6 months at Terme di Saturnia, Italy, honing his skills. He uses only fresh ingredients, no artificial sweeteners, no more than 3 grams of sugar in any recipe (which makes for diabetic-approved desserts), and there is never more than 20 percent fat in any meal. On the menu, each item is followed by its caloric, carbohydrate, and fat value, and a calculator is inserted into each menu. Several two- and three-course meals are also provided with numbers already calculated for those who don't want to be bothered figuring out totals for themselves. I was so impressed with Michael McVay's cooking that I have included four of his recipes, all taste-tested by me, for you to try. The three principles that make this food alone worth the trip are the rawness of technique, simplicity in combinations, and basic goodness of every ingredient.

GRILLED RASPBERRY CHICKEN
(Serves six)

¼ cup raspberry vinegar
2 tablespoons fresh basil
½ teaspoon black pepper
¼ teaspoon dry thyme

2 tablespoons chopped shallots
6 skinned breasts of chicken
*   ("free-range" or organically fed*
*   is best)*

GLAZE
1½ cups veal stock (you may
*   substitute chicken)*

¾ cup raspberry vinegar

Combine vinegar, basil, pepper, thyme, and shallots. Add chicken and marinate in refrigerator for 6 hours prior to cooking. While chicken is cooking, make glaze by combining veal stock with ¾ cup raspberry vinegar. Cook in skillet over low heat until reduced by half. Grill chicken breasts on open barbecue. Add remainder of marinade to reduced stock and vinegar. Bring to boil. Pour over finished chicken. 180 calories. Fiber, 4 grams. Sodium, 78 mg (per serving).

CANNELLONI WITH VEGETABLE FILLING
(Serves six)

VEGETABLE FILLING
1 cup grated onions
1 cup grated celery
1 cup grated zucchini
1 cup grated carrots
2 tablespoons chopped garlic
½ teaspoon salt (optional)
1 pinch pepper
2 teaspoons fresh chopped oregano

2 teaspoons fresh chopped basil
1 teaspoon fresh chopped thyme or ½ teaspoon dry thyme
8 ounces low-sodium 1 percent fat cottage cheese
1 ounce freshly grated Parmesan cheese
12 sheets (1 ounce each) whole wheat cannelloni pasta (about 6 inches × 6 inches cooked)

RED SAUCE
(Serves six)

1 can (28 ounces) crushed tomatoes
1 large carrot, peeled and chopped
1 medium onion, peeled and chopped

2 cups chicken stock, low sodium, no fat
4 cloves garlic, chopped
1 tablespoon fresh chopped basil

Preheat oven to 325°F. Place all vegetables and herbs for vegetable filling in a heavy saucepan. Cook over low heat until vegetables are tender. Remove from heat. Fold in cottage cheese and Parmesan cheese. Set aside. Cook pasta in 3 to 4 quarts boiling water until soft but still firm (1 to 2 minutes). Lay noodles out flat and fill with ¼ cup of the vegetable-cheese mixture. Roll up each noodle and place seam side down in a glass casserole dish. Cover tightly with aluminum foil. Heat for 25 minutes. Serve two rolls with ¼ cup heated red sauce. 280 calories per serving. Fiber, 4 grams. Sodium, 400 mg.

RED SAUCE
Simmer all ingredients in a heavy saucepan for 1 hour. Cool to room temperature. Puree in food processor or blender until smooth. Makes 5 ½ cups. A ¼-cup serving has 20 calories.

MUSHROOM AND GREEN PEPPER PIZZA
(Serves one)

3 ounces dough (follow recipe below)

2 tablespoons whole wheat flour

2 ounces red sauce (see recipe on page 136)

2 large mushrooms

3 rings of bell (or red or yellow) pepper

1 ounce buffalo milk cheese (can substitute low-fat mozzarella)

DOUGH
(Twelve servings)

1 package yeast

2 cups warm water

¹/₄ teaspoon salt

3 cups whole wheat flour, pastry grind

2¹/₂ cups unbleached white flour

DOUGH

Soften yeast in warm water. Combine salt and flours. Add 2 cups of the flour mixture to the yeast and water, stirring until smooth. Stir in as much of the remaining flour as you can mix in with a spoon. Turn out onto a lightly floured surface. Knead in enough of the remaining flour to make a fairly stiff dough that is smooth and elastic (knead for 6 to 8 minutes total). Shape into a ball. Place in a lightly greased bowl, turning once to grease surface, and cover. Let rise in a warm place until double in size (about 1 hour). Punch down.

Preheat oven to 400°F. Pat dough with the palms of your hands into a circle about 8 inches across. Sprinkle with flour. Spread sauce mixture evenly over the dough and top with vegetables and cheese. Bake 12 minutes on a cookie sheet.

290 calories

ARUGULA, ENDIVE, AND RADICCHIO SALAD
(Serves two)

1 small bunch arugula

1 small head endive

1 small head radicchio

1 pinch cracked black pepper

DRESSING
²/₃ cup red wine vinegar

¹/₂ cup olive oil

Arrange arugula, endive, and radicchio on plate. Sprinkle with cracked black pepper. Mix vinegar and oil together and shake vigorously. Pour 1 tablespoon dressing over salad.

30 calories per serving. Fiber, 0.6 grams. Sodium, 24 mg.

If you are in the mood for all-out luxury and pampering with the added benefit of a health and fitness resort, it would be hard to find anyplace better than the Doral Saturnia International Spa Resort.

CONCLUSION

I hope I have sparked your interest in body care and given you some workable suggestions to incorporate into your daily life. You will be amazed at the difference proper care will make in the appearance of your body. Seeing positive results makes it easy to continue a regimen. However, you may find it helpful to regard your desire for a beautiful, healthy body as more of a journey or quest than a finite, end result, because it is, in fact, exactly that. Don't be discouraged if a new problem appears soon after one problem has been solved. Instead of finding this to be disheartening, consider it a challenge and a way of continuing your education. After all, the more problems you have to solve, the more you'll have to learn, and the more you learn, the wiser and more beautiful you'll become.

About the Author

Zia Wesley-Hosford is a graduate of the Vidal Sassoon Academy in San Francisco and founder of the Zia Cosmetics Company. Her holistic approach to lasting good looks includes guidance on vitamins, nutrition, and exercise as well as skin care products. Her previous publications include BEING BEAUTIFUL (1983), PUTTING ON YOUR FACE: The Ultimate Guide to Cosmetics (1985), FACE VALUE: Skin Care for Women Over 35 (1986) and SKIN CARE FOR MEN ONLY (1987). Zia also publishes a quarterly newsletter, *Great Face*, which keeps readers informed of the latest research and innovations in skin products and treatments. She is a resident of San Francisco, CA.